SPEND THE DAY
IN ANCIENT ROME

SPEND THE DAY IN ANCIENT ROME

Projects and Activities
That Bring the Past to Life

Linda Honan

Illustrations by Ellen Kosmer

John Wiley & Sons, Inc.

New York • Chichester • Weinheim • Brisbane • Singapore • Toronto

Published by John Wiley & Sons, Inc.

Published simultaneously in Canada

The publisher and the author have made every reasonable effort to ensure that the experiments and activities in this book are safe when conducted as instructed but assume no responsibility for any damage caused or sustained while performing the experiments or activities in the book. Parents, guardians, and/or teachers should supervise young readers who undertake the experiments and activities in this book.

Library of Congress Cataloging-in-Publication Data

Honan, Linda.
    Spend the day in ancient Rome : projects and activities that bring the past to life / Linda Honan ; illustrated by Ellen Kosmer.

p.   cm.

ISBN 0-471-15453-9 (pbk. : alk. paper)

1. Rome—Social life and customs—Juvenile literature. 2. Rome—History—Empire, 30 B.C.–284 A.D.—Juvenile literature. 3. Rome—Civilization—Miscellanea—Juvenile literature.   I. Title.

DG78.H56   1998

937'.6—dc21   97-40681

Acknowledgments

I would like to thank my colleagues and friends at Higgins Armory Museum for their encouragement and forbearance. Particular thanks are due to our wonderful editorial team, Kate C. Bradford and John Simko, for all their help.

—L. H.

I appreciate the interest and encouragement of Bonnie Kind, who lent a hand in Nantucket. Her friendship and support have been invaluable. Many thanks to my friend and collaborator, Linda Honan, for bearing with my academic preoccupations, which frequently affected the schedule of illustrations.

—E. K.

CONTENTS

INTRODUCTION

Welcome to Ancient Rome!

Imagine you could travel back in time almost two thousand years to spend the day in ancient Rome, one of the greatest civilizations in history. This book will take you back to the city of Rome, capital of the Roman Empire, in the year A.D. 125. An empire is a large state made up of several countries and ruled by an **emperor.** You will visit Rome when the empire was at its most powerful and Emperor Hadrian was its ruler. To get to ancient Rome you took a ship to a port called Ostia, and then walked or rode fifteen miles (24 km) to the city. As you came closer you could see the seven hills of Rome shining in the sun.

Every September the people of Rome celebrated the success of their armies with a festival called the Ludi Romani (LOO-dee roh-MAHN-ee), or Roman Games. The festival lasted for two weeks. In this book you will visit Rome on September 13, a date the Romans called the Ides of September, when the games were in full swing. (The **ides** fell on the thirteenth or fifteenth of each month.) A big parade was followed by a gladiator show, chariot races, and music and entertainment at the theaters.

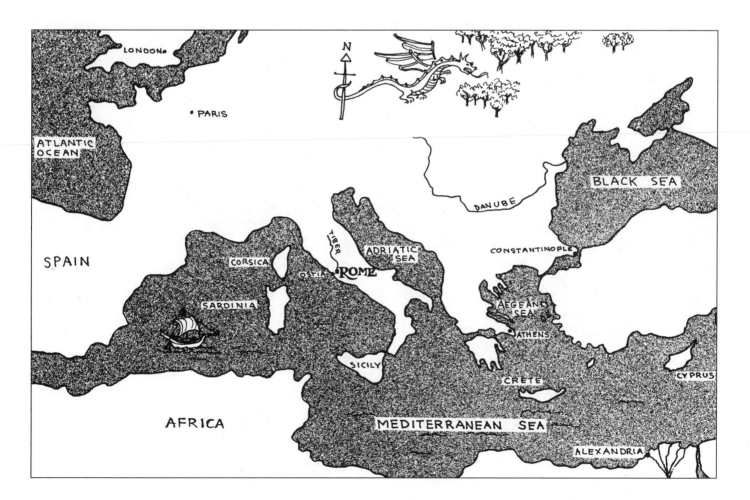

Two thousand years ago, the Roman Empire was the most powerful state in the world. From its capital, the city of Rome in Italy, the empire stretched all the way around the Mediterranean Sea, and included Greece, Israel, Egypt, Tunisia, Spain, Germany, and Britain. Over a hundred million people of different nationalities lived in the empire. They all obeyed Roman laws, worshipped the official gods of Rome, and spoke Latin, the official Roman language—even though many Romans spoke their own national language at home.

The state of Rome was founded in 753 B.C. as a small kingdom in central Italy. In 27 B.C. the Romans crowned Augustus (63 B.C.–A.D. 14, reigned 27 B.C.–A.D. 14) as their first emperor, creating the Roman Empire. This lasted until A.D. 476, when Goths and Vandals invaded Rome and destroyed the city and the empire. Roman law is the basis for much modern law. Roman scientists and **engineers** (people who design and build roads and buildings) made great discoveries, and their writers and historians wrote books that we still study today.

Meet the Family

You are going to spend the day with Senator Claudius Julius Flavius, his wife, Livia, and their children, twelve-year-old Julia and ten-year-old Marcus. The senator is usually called Julius. Like all rich Romans, Julius and Livia employ slaves to work for them. The slaves were either born to slave parents or captured during wars. Julius trusts Tullius to write all his letters and keep his accounts.

Tullius   Marcus   Julius   Julia   Claudia

Besides looking after the household, Livia earns money by buying and selling land and houses. Livia is helped in her work by Calpurnia, who is a friend as well as a servant.

Julia is very fond of her nanny, Claudia, while Marcus has mixed feelings for Jason, a learned Greek who is called his *pedagogue*. Jason brings Marcus to school each day, helps with homework, and still gives Julia lessons when she isn't with her mother, learning how to care for a family.

The family owns two other houses besides their main house in Rome. To keep cool in the hot Roman summers, they go out to their villa in the resort town of Tibur (TYE-bur)—called Tivoli today. The family also has a farm that produces their food.

The Projects and Activities

In this book, you'll follow Julia and Marcus through their day, and along the way you'll do many of the things that they did. You'll make the kinds of clothes and jewelry they wore, write the way they did, prepare the kind of food they ate, and much more. Through these projects and activities ancient Rome will come alive. And you'll discover what life was like for children—just like you—living thousands of years ago.

Guide to Latin Pronunciation

Latin pronunciation is easy. Each letter is sounded. Most consonants sound the same as they do in English. Note how the following consonants are sounded.

c is always sounded like the *c* in *cat*, never like the *c* in *city*.
g is always sounded like the *g* in *gate*, never like the *g* in *gem*.
h is always sounded like the *h* in *honey*; it is never silent like the *h* in *hour*.
i at the start of a word may be a consonant or a vowel; as a consonant it is pronounced
　　like the *y* in *yam*.
v is always sounded like the *w* in *want*, never like the *v* in *victor*.

Each Latin vowel has two sounds, long and short. In some words the vowel sound is short, and in others long. Latin dictionaries put a line called a **macron** over long vowels. Vowels are sounded as in the following list.

a short is sounded like *u* in *nut*.
a long is sounded like *a* in *father*.
e short is sounded like *e* in *pet*.
e long is sounded like *ey* in *they*.
i short is sounded like *i* in *sit*.
i long is sounded like *ee* in *deep*.
o short is sounded like *o* in *dot*.
o long is sounded like *o* in *note*.

u short is sounded like *u* in *put.*
u long is sounded like *oo* in *school.*
y as a vowel is sounded like *i* in *sit.*

Two vowels written next to each other and spoken as one sound are called a **diphthong.** Latin diphthongs are sounded as in the following list.

ae is sounded like *eye.*
au is sounded like *ow* in *cow.*
ei is sounded like *ay* in *day.*
oe is sounded like *oy* in *toy.*

Many Latin names of emperors and famous people are pronounced like English words. Some examples are Caesar (SEE-zur), Cicero (SISS-er-oh), Hadrian (HADE-ree-un), and Trajan (TRAY-jun).

CHAPTER·1

WAKING IN THE VILLA

Claudia goes from Julia's room to Marcus's room, shaking the children awake while it is still dark outside. The family has been spending the summer at their country house, or *villa*, in Tibur, in the hills outside Rome. Summer is ending, and today they must return to the city.

Half asleep, they get out of bed and dress. Julia puts on a long gown, called a *stola*, and Marcus puts on a knee-length tunic. Each of them wears a gold charm, called a *bulla*, around the neck, for protection against bad luck. In the kitchen, the children each eat a bread roll and drink some milk. Then they hurry out to the garden,

where their
parents, Julius
and Livia,
along with
their ser-
vants, are
bundling
their
belong-
ings into
oxcarts for
the journey
back to Rome.

ACTIVITY

STOLA

In this activity you'll make a stola, the kind of tunic that Roman
women and older girls wore. The Roman stola was made of a
straight piece of linen or woolen cloth, pinned at the shoulders,
with a big collar hanging down nearly to the waist.

MATERIALS

scissors
sheet, tablecloth, or fabric remnant at least 6 x 5 feet (2 x 1.75 m)
yardstick (meterstick)
2 diaper pins or large safety pins
2-to-3-foot (60-to-90-cm) length of rope

1. Cut your cloth to a piece 6 x 5 feet (2 x 1.75 m).
Fold over the top 18 inches (45 cm) of the cloth as shown
on page 7.

2. Fold the cloth in half the long way as shown below.

3. Leave a hole for your head in the middle, and fasten a pin at each shoulder.

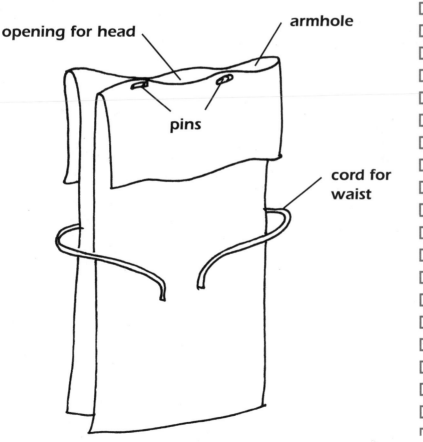

opening for head

armhole

pins

cord for waist

If you met some people on the streets of ancient Roman, you would have thought they all wore the same kind of clothes! Whether you were a man or a woman, a boy or a girl, you wore the same thing—a tunic, with a cloak over it in cold weather. Women, teenage girls, and old men wore a tunic down to their ankles. Children and most men wore a shorter one down to the knees. For formal events, men wore a special woolen cloak, called a **toga,** over their tunics.

Your clothes were made of wool or linen, which housewives and servants spun into cloth. If you were rich you could buy imported silk and have it made into clothes. Your clothes were dyed various colors with vegetable dyes. The most expensive dye was purple, which was made from the murex seashell. This was used to make the stripe on togas, and clothes for the emperor.

4. Put on the stola, then tie the rope around your waist for a belt.

5. Pull the cloth up above the belt, so the stola ends at your ankles.

ACTIVITY

TUNICA EXTERIOR

The usual dress of children and men in Rome was a knee-length tunic called a **tunica exterior.** The tunic was sleeveless or had short sleeves. Tunics were made of wool or linen, and were usually white. Roman soldiers wore a brick-red knee-length tunic under their armor. Romans usually belted their tunics with a leather or woolen belt. Make your own tunica exterior in the next activity.

MATERIALS
72-by-36-inch (180-by-90-cm) unpatterned
  sheet, tablecloth, or length of fabric
yardstick (meterstick)
scissors
1-yard (90-cm) length of rope

1. Fold the cloth in half, so it is 1 yard (90 cm) long.

2. Cut an 8-inch (20-cm)-wide opening for your head at the fold.

3. Put the tunic on and tie the rope around your waist for a belt.

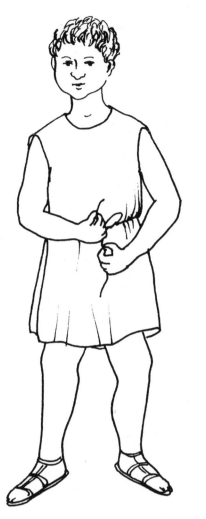

ACTIVITY
BULLA

Roman children wore a charm called a bulla for protection against bad luck. It was a gold pendant charm with a raised crescent moon on it. Children in southern Italy still wear a similar charm made of gold or coral. In this activity you can make your own bulla.

MATERIALS

several sheets of newspaper
¼ pound (125 g) of self-hardening clay, about the size of a plum

pencil
craft stick or modeling tool
jar of water
paintbrush (optional)
gold or brown poster paint (optional)
18-inch (45-cm) length of cord or string

1. Spread the newspaper over your work area.

2. Work the clay in your hands until it is soft and warm. Pull off a small piece of clay about the size of the tip of your little finger. Set the small piece aside.

3. Roll the remaining clay on the newspaper into a round shape like a big marble. Flatten it into a circle ¼ inch (0.6 cm) thick—about as thick as the pencil.

4. Smooth the surface of the clay with the craft stick or your fingers to remove any holes or lines.

5. Take the small piece of clay you set aside in step 2. Shape it into a crescent moon as shown.

6. Dip your finger in the water jar, and wet the back of the crescent. Place the crescent in the center of your big piece of clay, with the wet side down and the ends of the crescent pointing up. Press it gently so it sticks.

7. Use the craft stick to gently press a circle all around the edge of the bulla.

8. Use the pencil to push a hole through the bulla near the center top.

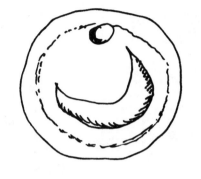

9. Leave the bulla on a piece of clean newspaper while it is drying, as it will leave a stain while wet. Let it dry for 2 days indoors, away from radiators, sunny windows, or other sources of heat.

10. (Optional) When the bulla is dry, paint it gold or brown.

11. Run the cord through the hole in the bulla and tie the ends in a knot. Now wear your bulla around your neck!

CHAPTER·2
GOOD-BYE TO TIBUR

Both Julia and Marcus are sad to be leaving the villa where they have spent the summer. Julia touches the flowers growing beside the big pool. Marcus runs over to the stables to say good-bye to the horses.

Senator Julius gives a signal and the first wagon moves off, with Julius, Livia, Tullius, and Calpurnia. Julia and Marcus are in the second wagon with Claudia and Jason. As their wagon moves slowly down the path, Julia and Marcus look back at the beautiful gardens and house. Some children with whom they have played all summer have come to see them off. Julia and Marcus wave good-bye to them. As they turn the corner onto the road, the last thing Julia sees is the sign on the wall warning visitors, CAVE CANEM (KAH-way KAH-num), which means "Beware of the dog."

The wagons roll along the road as quickly as they can. They must arrive in Rome before daylight. A new law forbids any wagons from entering the city during the day, to keep the streets from becoming too crowded.

Both children wave until the villa is out of sight, then they settle back in their blankets. They will miss Tibur, with its animals and swimming pool and games in the garden—but the winter in Rome will be full of excitement!

Julia and Marcus's father, Julius, decides when the family will return to Rome. Julius is called the paterfamilias because he is the oldest man in the family. As paterfamilias, he makes all the important decisions for the whole family. When Julia and Marcus were born, Julius had to inspect them and decide whether to leave them outside to die or to take them in and raise them.

Like other children, Juila and Marcus have to do what their parents tell them, although their mother has no legal rights over her children. Like all Roman women, Livia spends her whole life under the control of a man—first her father, then her husband. On the other hand, Roman women work in many

COUNTRY MOUSE AND TOWN MOUSE

The Roman writer Horace (65–8 B.C.) compared life in town and in the country in his story of a country mouse. A friend from town came to visit the country mouse. The country mouse welcomed the town mouse into his little house and shared his simple supper with his friend.

The town mouse found the country too rough. He invited the country mouse back to the city to see its luxuries. While they ate a fancy supper in town, they were disturbed by a pack of barking dogs. As they ran for their lives, the country mouse said, "No thanks. Life may be simple in the country, but it's nice and peaceful, and I'm going back there." (Horace, **Satires** 2.6.79)

professions and businesses. Julia plans to buy and sell real estate, as Livia does. Julia hopes to make a lot of money, as her mother has done.

When Julius and Marcus decide they want to marry, they will have to get Julius's permission. Marcus will also have to ask permission to join the legions, or to go to Athens to study, or to go into business. As long as Julius lives, he will be their paterfamilias!

ACTIVITY

WALL SIGN

The Romans had many signs painted on the plaster walls of their houses. People sometimes scratched messages on them, too— MARIUS CLAUDIAM AMAT (MARIUS LOVES CLAUDIA), for example. You can make your own Latin sign and put it on the refrigerator or wall. You can use one of the Latin sayings listed here. Or you can ask at your library if your state or city motto is in Latin, and then use it for your sign. Write your saying in capital letters, which is how the Romans wrote.

LATIN SAYINGS

Ad astra To the stars (motto of the United States Air Force)

Cave canem Beware of the dog

Cave felicem (KAH-way feh-LEEK-em) Beware of the cat

E pluribus unum One out of many (motto of the United States, found on coins and on the dollar bill)

Lux et veritas Light and truth (motto of Yale University)

Semper fidelis Always faithful (motto of the United States Marine Corps)

Semper paratus Always prepared (motto of the United States Coast Guard)

MATERIALS

pencil
ruler
6-by-8-inch (15-by-20-cm) piece of cardboard
one-hole paper punch
Latin Sayings list
black marker
18-inch (45-cm) length of string

1. Mark a point 1 inch (2.5 cm) in from each of the top corners of the cardboard. Punch a hole at each of these points.

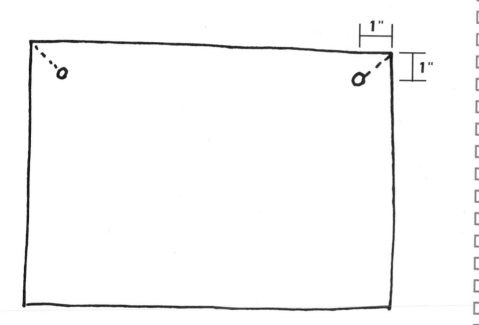

2. Choose a Latin saying from the list, or use your state or city motto. Use the pencil to print your saying on the cardboard.

3. Draw a border around your saying. Copy the design as shown on page 16 to make your border look Roman.

LATIN

The language of ancient Rome is Latin. The name "Latin" comes from the state of Latium (LAH-tee-oom) in central Italy, where the early Romans lived. When the ancient Romans defeated other nations, they taught them to speak and write Latin. So as the empire grew, many Romans spoke two languages—their own national language and Latin. Ancient Rome became an empire of many cultures and languages.

Latin is the official language of the Roman Catholic Church, and Catholics spread the language throughout the world. Scholars and lawyers wrote and spoke Latin until the eighteenth century. English and other languages have adopted many words from Latin. In Italy, where Latin was once spoken, the people now speak Italian, a language that developed from Latin. Many people still study Latin, but no nation speaks Latin today.

4. Go over the saying and the border with the marker.

5. Tie the ends of the string through each of the holes. Find a good place to hang your sign!

ACTIVITY

ROMAN BOYS' NAMES

Every man who was a Roman citizen had at least two names: a **praenomen,** which was his personal name, and a **nomen,** which was his family name. For example, the praenomen of Marcus Tullius Cicero, the great Roman writer, was Marcus, and his nomen was Tullius. The praenomen of Gaius Julius Caesar, the Roman leader, was Gaius, and his nomen was Julius.

Many Roman men added a third name after the first two. This third name was the **cognomen,** which was their clan name, or nickname. For example, the cognomen of Marcus Tullius Cicero was Cicero, which was the nickname given to his branch of the Tullius family. (Cicero means "chickpea," and one of his ancestors had warts!) The cognomen of Gaius Julius Caesar was Caesar.

Within a family, a boy was called by his praenomen—for example, Marcus—but everyone else called him by his nomen or cognomen: Tullius or Cicero. One reason for this was that there were only about twenty different personal names. So whenever a crowd of Romans gathered, there would be many different people with the same praenomen.

Choose a Roman boy's name for yourself in this activity. You can choose a Latin praenomen from the Latin Boys' Personal Names list, or change your own first name to sound like a Latin praenomen. You can also change your family name to sound like a Latin nomen. Add a nickname as your cognomen if you like!

For example, if your name is Paul Smith, you could change your name to Paulus Smithus. If you are a fast runner, you may want to add a cognomen that means "quick." Look in a Latin dictionary to find a word that means "fast." Then your full Latin name might be Paulus Smithus Celeriter.

LATIN BOYS' PERSONAL NAMES

Augustus (Magnificent)

Benedictus (Blessed)

Clarentius (Famous)

Dexter (Right)

Felix (Happy)

Leo (Lion)

Patricius (Noble)

Petrus (Rock)

Rex (King)

Victor (Winner)

MATERIALS

Latin Boys' Personal Names list

Latin dictionary (optional)

pencil

black marker

sheet of paper or wall sign from previous activity

1. Change your first name by adding -*us* or -*ius* to the end so that it sounds Roman, or pick one of the names listed here.

2. Change your family name by adding -*us* or -*ius* to the end so that it sounds Roman.

3. (Optional) Decide on a nickname. Look up the word you want in a Latin dictionary.

4. Use the pencil to write out your Roman name in capital letters. Go over your name with the marker. If you like, write it on the wall sign from the previous activity!

PAULUS SMITHUS CELERITER

ACTIVITY

ROMAN GIRLS' NAMES

Roman women had only one name throughout their lives: it was their father's nomen, with the feminine ending -*a*. For example, Gaius Julius Caesar's daughter was called Julia, and Marcus Tullius Cicero's daughter was called Tullia.

If a father had more than one daughter, a word was added to show that a daughter was elder, or younger, or the first or second or third daughter, and so on. For example, Caesar's eldest daughter would have been called Julia Maior (Julia the Elder) or Julia Prima (Julia the First), and his second daughter would have been called Julia Minor (Julia the Younger) or Julia Secunda (Julia the Second).

After Roman times, people in many countries gave their daughters a Latin word as a name. Instead of using your family name for your Roman name, you may choose a Latin word from the list here.

WORDS TO DESCRIBE A DAUGHTER'S PLACE IN THE FAMILY

Maior (MY-or) (Elder)	Tertia (Third)
Minor (Younger)	Quarta (Fourth)
Prima (First)	Quinta (Fifth)
Secunda (Second)	Sexta (Sixth)

LATIN WORDS USED AS GIRLS' NAMES

Amanda (Beloved)
Carmen (Song)
Clara (Bright)
Diana (Goddess of the Hunt)
Dolores (Sad)
Gloria (Glorious)

Regina (Queen)
Stella (Star)
Sylvia (Forest)
Vera (True)
Victoria (Victorious)

MATERIALS

list of Words to Describe a Daughter's Place in the Family
list of Latin Words Used as Girls' Names
pencil
black marker
sheet of paper or wall sign from previous activity

1. Change your family name by adding *-a* or *-ia* to the end so that it sounds Roman, or pick a name from the list here.

2. Find the Latin word for your place in the family from the list of words.

3. Use the pencil to write out your Roman name in capital letters. Go over your name with the marker. If you like, write it on the wall sign from the earlier activity!

JULIUS CAESAR

The great Roman general and politician Gaius Julius Caesar was killed by his friend Brutus and other senators in 44 B.C. The senators killed Caesar because they were afraid that he had become too popular and might want to make himself their emperor.

Caesar was a clever general who won many battles. He wrote a great history of his wars. After one quick expedition, he sent back a three-word message to Rome: "Veni, vidi, vici" (I came, I saw, I conquered).

JULIA SECUNDA

CHAPTER·3

AT HOME IN ROME

Julia holds on tight to the wagon as it rolls through the big gates and into the city of Rome. Suddenly the noise and activity of Rome surround them— there are about a million people living in the city. Julia and Marcus live in a big house in the center of Rome, not far from the emperor's palace on the Palatine Hill. From the street they can see the long yellow wall of their house, with one big door and a red tiled roof. They tumble out of the wagon and hurry inside.

Everything is just as Julia and Marcus remember. Inside the door they step into the atrium. The *atrium* is an entrance hall with an open roof and a shallow pool that collects rainwater. The pool is called an *impluvium*. Marcus dips his hand in the impluvium—the water is warm, not like the cool, deep swimming pool at Tibur.

Marcus runs through the house, checking on everything. The house is colorful, with floors covered with marble or tiles. The walls are decorated with marble or painted with big pictures called *murals*. Julius is in his study, called the *tablinum*. Marcus looks in at the dining room, called the *triclinium*, where three sofas are arranged around a table. Then he hears voices in the kitchen. His mother, Livia, is there, talking with Calpurnia and the cook. Marcus hears Jason calling him, and runs away to the courtyard behind the atrium.

The courtyard is called the *peristyle* (PER-ee-stile), and only the family or very close friends use it. The kitchen and some bedrooms open onto the peristyle, and marble stairs lead up to other bedrooms on the second floor. Marcus sees Julia in the peristyle, having her hair done by her nanny, Claudia. Julia is sitting on the edge of a fishpond in which goldfish are swimming. A fountain in the fishpond gives off a cooling spray and makes a pleasant sound.

ROMAN HOUSES

The streets of ancient Rome were lined with large houses. Many of them were six stories high, built of brick and cement. These were apartment houses, called **insulae**, or islands, where many families lived. They were dark and hot and smoky, because there were very few windows. Some insulae had toilets in the basement. Otherwise the people had to use the public toilets outside.

Senators and other rich people lived on the hills, in large houses built of stone or brick. These houses looked plain from the outside. They had few windows in the outer wall and only one door, to keep the family safe from robbers. But inside they were luxurious, with big rooms filled with furniture and decorated with art. There was a garden at the back. Some rich people had a bathroom with water piped in. A rich Roman's house was big enough to house his family, guests, and hundreds of slaves.

ACTIVITY

MOSAIC DESIGN

Many Roman floors were covered with hundreds of small tiles, called **tesserae.** The tesserae were made from cubes of stone, so their colors were natural stone colors: gray, brown, green, brick red, white, or tan. A **mosaic** is a design or picture made by arranging the tesserae in a pattern. In this activity you'll use beans to make your own mosaic design.

MATERIALS

pencil
ruler
12-inch (30-cm) -square piece of corrugated cardboard
drawing compass
1 pound (0.5 kg) dry beans in a dark color, such as black beans or
*   red chili beans*
1 pound (0.5 kg) dry beans in a light color, such as pinto beans or
*   baby lima beans*
white glue

1. Use the pencil and ruler to draw a diagonal line from corner to corner on the cardboard square. Draw another diagonal line between the other corners. The point where these lines cross is the center point.

2. Put the point of the drawing compass on the center point and draw a 4-inch (10-cm) circle on the cardboard square.

3. Use the pencil and ruler to draw a line across the cardboard square 1 inch (2.5 cm) down from the top.

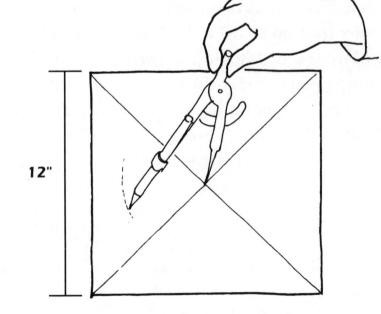

4. Repeat step 3 on the other three sides of the cardboard square to make a border around the circle.

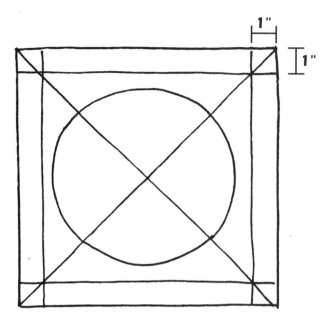

5. Take a dark bean, and put a drop of glue on it. Place this bean at the center point of the design. Continue to fill in the design with the other dark beans, using the picture here as a guide.

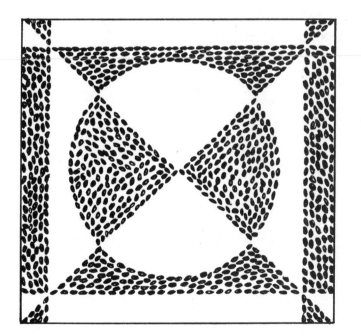

6. When you've glued all of the dark beans to the cardboard, fill in the design with the light beans.

ROMULUS AND REMUS

The ancient Romans believed in an old legend, or story, that their nation was founded by twin brothers named Romulus and Remus. The city of Rome is named for Romulus. The story tells that when the twins were babies, a wicked king put them in a basket and dropped them in a river called the Tiber. But the basket floated to shore, and the boys were rescued by a female wolf. The wolf nursed them and kept them safe until they were grown. Because of this legend, the symbol for the modern city of Rome is a wolf. To this day, wolves live in a cage on a hill called the Capitoline in the middle of the city of Rome!

ACTIVITY

MOSAIC PICTURE

In addition to making mosaic designs on their floors, the
Romans covered many of their walls with mosaic pictures. In
earlier centuries the Romans made their mosaic pictures in the
muted colors of natural stone. In later centuries they added
cubes of brightly colored glass and gemstones to their mosaic
pictures. In this activity you can make a mosaic picture using
construction paper in the soft colors of natural stone.

MATERIALS

pencil
ruler
six 8½-by-11-inch (21.5-by-27.5-cm) sheets of construction paper,
   one each of the following colors: brown, green, brick red, white,
   tan, gray
scissors
12-by-18-inch (30-by-45-cm) piece of gray, black, or brown poster
   board
white glue

1. Use the pencil and ruler to mark ½-inch (1.25-cm) squares
on one sheet of construction paper. Cut out the squares. Keep all
the squares in one pile.

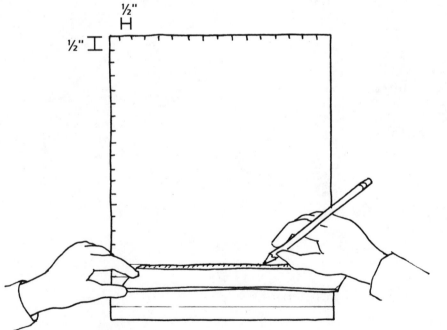

2. Repeat step 1 with the other five sheets of construction paper. Keep the six colored piles separate from one another.

3. Use the pencil to draw a picture of your home on the poster board. Draw a simple outline without many details, as shown in the picture.

4. Decide which colors to use to fill in the picture of your home. For example, will the walls be white? Or red? Or tan? Will the roof be gray? Or brown? Or red? Will the windows be white? Or green?

5. Put a dot of glue on the back of a square and glue it on the poster board. Glue down the other squares, leaving ⅛ inch (0.3 cm) between each of the squares.

½"

enlargement of picture on page 25

CHAPTER 4

HONORING THE GODS

A s the servants unload the wagons, Julius calls the family together. They must honor the gods, to give thanks for their safe journey, and to ask for a blessing. Julia and Marcus join their parents in the atrium. They have a family shrine there. This is a cupboard with statues of the gods who watch over their family. The shrine is called the *lararium*. Julius has put on the toga that Roman men wear for important business. As paterfamilias, he must lead them all in prayer each day.

At the back of the atrium there is a sacred hearth with a fire that burns every day, winter and summer. As the mother of the family, Livia must keep the fire in this hearth always burning. They believe that if the fire

goes out, disaster
will come to the
family.

For this cer-
emony Livia
is wearing a
beautiful
stola and
glittering
gold earrings.
She puts wood
on the fire, and
Julius throws a salt
cake in it, as an offering

to the gods. Julia and Marcus bow their heads in
prayer. After praying to their own household gods,
Julius offers prayers to Jupiter, Juno, and Minerva,
the gods in whose honor the Roman Games are
being held.

Julius and Marcus worship their own household
gods every day. They honor two kinds of household
gods, the gods of the hearth and the gods of the
pantry. The gods of the hearth are called the Lares,
and they keep the family safe. The gods of the
pantry are called the Penates, and they make sure
that the family always has enough food.

Livia teaches the children that a whole family of
gods keeps the state of Rome safe and gives success
or failure to each person in Rome. The Roman gods
are the same as the Greek gods, but they have different names. The head Roman god is Jupiter, who
is like the Greek god Zeus. Jupiter's wife and the
queen of the Roman gods is Juno, who is the same
as the Greek Hera. The god of war is Mars in Rome
and Ares in Greece. The goddess of wisdom is
Minerva in Rome and Athena in Greece.

ACTIVITY

EARRINGS

Roman girls and women enjoyed wearing large pieces of jewelry made of gold and colorful jewels. You can make a copy of Julia's favorite gold earrings, using dangling golden beads and a brightly colored glass jewel. Choose the color of the glass gem you'll add to these earrings!

MATERIALS

drawing compass
pencil
ruler
piece of thin cardboard, at least 1½ x 3 inches (3.75 x 7.5 cm)
    (Part of a cereal box works well.)
scissors
2 yards (2 m) golden or yellow cord (from a craft supply store)
stapler
1½-by-8-inch (3.75-by-20-cm) nonplasticized gold foil (from a florist) or aluminum foil
transparent tape
10 golden beads—2 large, 4 medium, 4 small (from a craft supply store)
glue gun (optional) or white glue
2 colored-glass gems with one flat side (from a craft supply store)
adult helper for glue gun

1. Use the drawing compass and pencil to make two small circles on the cardboard, each 1½ inches (3.75 cm) in diameter (the width of the circle). Use the scissors to cut them out.

1½"

2. Cut a 10½-inch (26-cm) length of cord. Place the cord on one of the cardboard circles as shown. The top loop of cord should extend above the cardboard 2½ inches (6.25 cm). The bottom loop of cord should extend below the cardboard ½ inch (1.25 cm). Staple the cord loops to the cardboard using four staples. The side of the cardboard with the cord will be the back of the earring.

3. Use the scissors to cut the foil into two pieces, each 1½ x 4 inches (3.75 x10 cm).

4. Cover one of the cardboard circles with one piece of foil. Tape the ends of the foil together on the back of the cardboard, covering the cord.

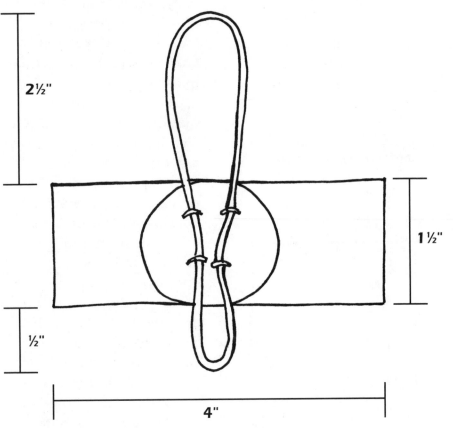

5. Cut five pieces of cord, each 5 inches (12.5 cm) long. Tie a double knot at one end of each piece of cord.

6. Thread a large golden bead on one piece of cord so it stops at the knotted end. Tie the other end of this cord to the middle of the ½-inch (1.25-cm) loop of cord hanging below the cardboard.

7. Repeat step 6 with two pieces of cord and two medium beads. Tie these cords shorter than the first cord so the beads hang above and on either side of the large bead.

8. Repeat step 6 with the remaining two pieces of cord and two small beads. Tie these cords a little shorter than you tied the cords in step 7 so the beads hang above and to the outside of the medium beads.

9. Have an adult helper use the glue gun to fasten a glass gem to the center front of the cardboard, or glue it on with white glue.

10. Repeat steps 2–9 to make the other earring. Now hang the earrings over your ears!

As well as praying to the gods each day, Julia and Marcus and their parents never start any new project without first checking the omens. The omens were signs that the Romans believed could tell the future. When the family was planning any important move, Livia would hire a fortune-teller called a *haruspex*, who was trained to interpret the omens. The haruspex would sacrifice a sheep in order to inspect its liver. The Romans believed the liver represented the universe. If the liver was healthy, your fortune would be good. But if it was unhealthy, the haruspex would tell you not to start out on the project.

ACTIVITY

TOGA

Men who were citizens of Rome wore a toga for all important occasions. The toga was made of a semicircle of white wool, and it was worn over a knee-length tunic. For some religious ceremonies, a man pulled the top part of the toga up over his head. A **senator,** an elected official who helped govern Rome, had a reddish-purple stripe along one side of his toga, as did a young boy.

Roman women and older girls wore a cloak draped like a toga, but without the purple stripe. Called a **palla,** the cloak could be any color and could have stripes along the border. Women and girls wore a stola under the palla. When they were outside, women and girls usually pulled the top of the palla over their heads like a veil. Wear your toga over a long white or red T-shirt.

MATERIALS
3 yards (3 m) of 3-inch (7.5-cm)-wide purple ribbon
white sheet, twin size or larger
stapler
helper

1. Place the ribbon along one edge of the sheet, from top to bottom.

2. Staple the ribbon to the sheet.

3. Drape your toga as shown in the picture. Start by draping the sheet over your left shoulder, with the ribboned side close to your neck. Adjust the sheet so it falls to your ankles in front.

4. Have your helper take all of the sheet that falls down your back and fold it up under your right arm, then over your left arm. Bend your left arm to catch and hold the toga in place. Now you can see why Romans wore the toga only for formal occasions!

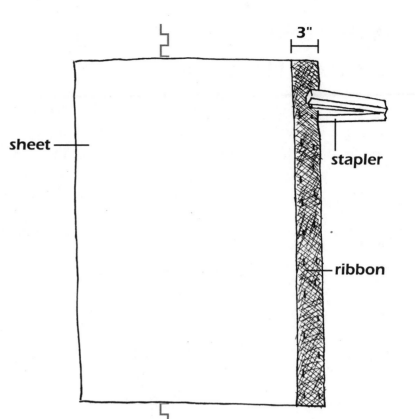

3"

sheet

stapler

ribbon

ACTIVITY

LARARIUM

Each Roman family had a lararium where they prayed each day. The lararium was a cupboard hanging on the wall, which held statues of the household gods. At the front of the lararium was a carving of a snake, which stood for the family's special spirit, called a **genius.** In this activity, you will make your own lararium.

MATERIALS

several sheets of newspaper
family-size cereal box
ruler
pencil
scissors
stapler
two 1¼-by-8-inch (3-by-20-cm) strips of white typing paper
9-by-7-inch (23-by-17.5-cm) piece of white paper
acrylic paint in various colors
paintbrushes
jar of water
white glue

1. Spread the newspaper over your work area.

2. On the front of the box, measure in 1¼ inch (3 cm) from each side. Draw a line up the front at each of these points.

3. Measure 1 inch (2.5 cm) up from the bottom of the box. Draw a line across the bottom front at this point.

4. Measure 2 inches (5 cm) down from the top of the box. Draw a line across the top front at this point.

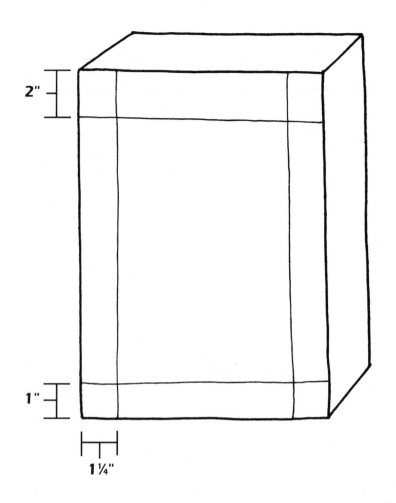

5. Cut out the rectangle you have drawn. Set the lararium (the rest of the box) aside.

6. Make the **pediment** (a triangle at the top center of the lararium):

a. On the cardboard rectangle, measure a smaller rectangle 8 x 5½ inches (20 x 14 cm) and cut it out. Set aside the extra cardboard.

b. On one long side of the small rectangle, measure the center point, 4 inches (10 cm) in from each end. Mark this point on the top edge of the cardboard.

c. On the short sides of the small rectangle, measure a point 1 inch (2.5 cm) up from the bottom on each side. Mark these points.

d. Draw a triangle connecting the center and side points. Cut out the pediment along your lines.

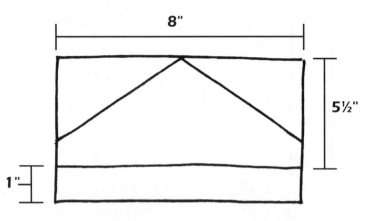

7. Cut a 1-by-8-inch (2.5-by-20-cm) strip from the extra card-board. Staple the strip across the bottom front of the lararium, gray side out.

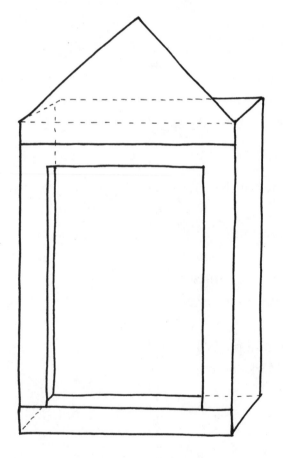

8. Make the columns and capitals (**columns** are pillars that support a roof; **capitals** are the top part of the column on which the roof rests). Take the two strips of white paper, and draw columns and capitals on them, as shown in the drawing. Staple the strips to the front sides of the lararium.

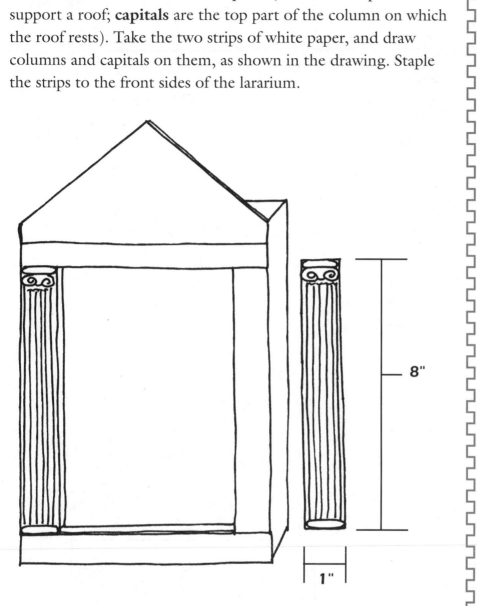

VESTAL VIRGINS

Just as Roman families kept the fire burning in their homes to keep the household gods happy, the whole empire of Rome was protected by a sacred fire burning in the Temple of Vesta, goddess of the hearth. This temple was in the center of the city of Rome. The temple fire was tended by important priestesses called the **Vestal Virgins.**

9. Staple the pediment from step 6 across the top front of the lararium, gray side out.

10. Draw a design of your family gods on the sheet of 9-by-7-inch (23-by-17.5-cm) paper. You can copy the design shown on page 38, or draw your own design.

11. Use the paints and brush to color your picture, and allow it to dry.

12. When the paint is dry, glue your picture to the inside back of the lararium.

13. Draw a snake, for the household genius, on the remaining cardboard and cut it out.

14. Paint the snake, and allow it to dry. When it is dry, glue it to the bottom front of the lararium.

15. Paint the outer sides and top of the lararium.

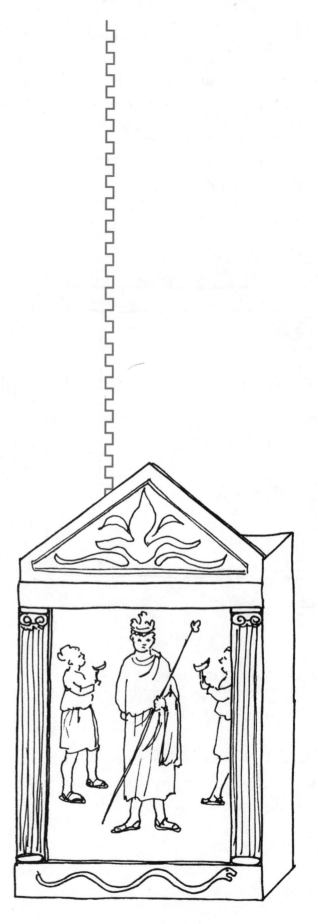

CHAPTER·5

MARCUS IN A PARADE

Before Marcus's time, the Roman *legions*, or armies, returned to Rome each September to spend the winter at home. In memory of this, boys in Marcus's day still dress up in armor and march through the city in a parade. Jason helps Marcus put on a helmet, cuirass (armored jacket), and a shield like the ones Marcus's father, Julius, wore when he was an officer in the legions. Jason also gives Marcus the *standard*, or badge, of his father's legion to carry.

When Marcus is ready, he runs to the tablinum to show Julius his armor. Then Marcus and Jason set off for the central square of Rome, called the *forum*. The forum is where the parade will begin. Marcus finds a couple of his friends to march with. The boys line up and start marching down the street called the Via Sacra, or Sacred Way.

Marcus marches smartly to the music of the trumpets and drums in the band. Some of the people who line the streets throw flowers to him. As Marcus catches the flowers in his left hand, he forgets how heavy his armor and the standard are. He waves the flowers at the cheering crowd. The crowd is happy that the real *legionaries*, or Roman soldiers, are victorious, and they are ready to enjoy a day of games and celebrations in honor of Jupiter.

As he marches, Marcus imagines what it must be like to be a real legionary. All the legionaries are volunteers, and Marcus means to join up when he is old enough. He knows that the Roman legions are the greatest army in the world. For many Roman men, joining the legions is a fine career. In return for twenty years' service, they are given a piece of land on which they can retire and farm.

Marcus doesn't mean to spend his whole life in the legions. Like his father, he wants to go into politics. He knows he will be able to win votes if he can tell people about his brave service as a legionary. Marcus can plan to join the legions because he is a Roman citizen. Slaves and foreigners could not join the army. If Marcus lived in one of the countries captured by Rome, he could join the *auxiliaries,* soldiers who worked with the legions and helped them.

As a legionary, Marcus will have to be not only a good fighter but also a skilled engineer. As well as fighting battles and keeping order, the legionaries build roads, bridges, towns, and temples all over the Roman Empire. Their roads are straight and level, cutting through hills, and are surfaced with stone. They build so well that some of their roads are still used today. Because of all the building they do, the legionaries have to carry a lot of gear with them—hammers, shovels, pickaxes. They carry so much that they are called "Marius's Mules," since Marius is a famous general in the legions. As Marcus thinks of all the things the real legionaries have to carry, he plans to start lifting weights the next time he goes to the exercise room at the bathhouse!

ACTIVITY

LEGIONARY'S SHIELD

One of the most important things every legionary carried was his shield. Tall and rectangular, the shield was made of wood and leather. It had a bronze **boss,** which was a central raised part in front of the handle.

When the legionaries attacked an enemy, they lined up in rows with their shields overlapping, so that they were completely protected. The rows of shields hiding the soldiers looked like the plated shell of a tortoise. This battle lineup was called the **testudo,** which means tortoise.

You can decorate your shield in the ancient Romans' favorite colors, red and yellow. Many legionary shields showed a thunderbolt, symbol of Jupiter, the greatest of the gods.

SOLDIERS AND ENGINEERS

If you needed to travel in ancient Rome, you were very grateful to the legionaries who built such good roads throughout the empire. As soon as the legionaries had captured a new province, they immediately started to build roads and bridges all across the territory. The next thing they built was a town, where the legion's officers could live. In each town they built a temple, a forum, an arena, and a bathhouse. To fill the baths, they brought water from a lake or spring. If the water source was far away, they built an aqueduct so the water could flow into the town. Two aqueducts built in the provinces by the legions that are still standing are the Pont du Gard near Nîmes in the south of France and the aqueduct at Segovia in Spain.

MATERIALS

pencil

ruler

2 pieces of corrugated cardboard, one piece 3 x 1½ feet (90 x 45 cm), and the other piece 9 x 7 inches (23 x 17.5 cm)

drawing compass

scissors

½-by-12-inch (1.25-by-30-cm) piece of sewing elastic or cardboard

4 brass brads

masking tape

white glue

3-by-1½-foot (90-by-45-cm) sheet of red construction paper

9-by-7-inch (23-by-17.5-cm) sheet of black construction paper

thumbtack

15-by-8-inch (37.5-by-20-cm) sheet of yellow construction paper

extra yellow construction paper (optional)

1. Use the pencil and ruler to draw a diagonal line from corner to corner on the big piece of cardboard. Draw another diagonal line between the other corners. Mark the center point where the lines cross. This piece of cardboard will be the shield.

2. Repeat step 1 with the small piece of cardboard. This will be the boss, the raised central part of the shield.

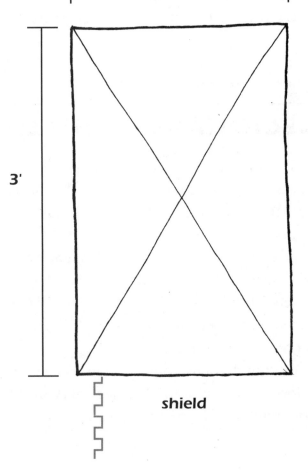

shield

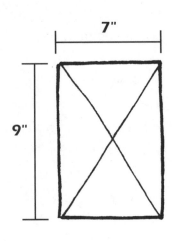

boss

3. Make the arm grip:

a. Lay the shield down with the pencil marks faceup. This side will be the back of the shield.

b. Place your arm across the center of the shield. Mark a dot on the cardboard on either side of your wrist and forearm as shown.

c. Use the pointed end of the drawing compass to make holes through each of the four dots.

d. Cut the elastic or cardboard strip into two pieces, one 7 inches (17.5 cm) long and one 5 inches (12.5 cm) long. Use the pointed end of the compass to make a hole in each end of the strips.

e. Lift up the shield and hold the smaller piece of elastic against the back of the shield where your wrist goes. Push each brad through the hole in the cardboard and the hole in the elastic. Open the ends of the brads to secure the elastic to the shield as shown.

f. Repeat step 3e to fasten the larger elastic where your forearm goes.

g. Cover the ends of the brads on the front of the shield with masking tape.

4. Cover the shield:

a. Turn the shield over, and squeeze a thin line of glue all over the front, in a spiral shape.

b. Stick the red construction paper on the shield.

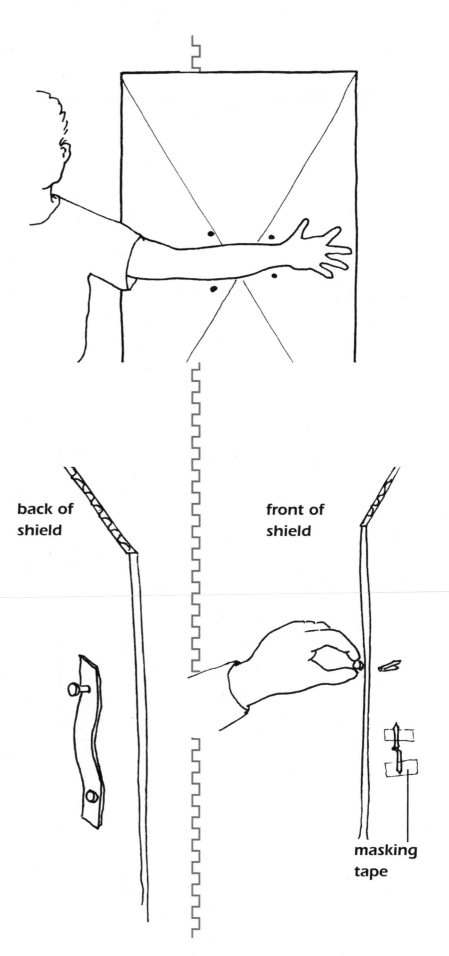

back of shield

front of shield

masking tape

5. Make the boss:

a. Lay the small piece of cardboard faceup. (The pencil lines should be on the back.)

b. Squeeze a thin line of glue all over the front, in a spiral shape.

c. Stick the black construction paper on the boss.

6. Fasten the boss to the shield:

a. Push the thumbtack through the center point of the shield, from back to front.

b. Take the boss and squeeze a thin line of glue all over the back, in a spiral shape.

c. Place the center point of the boss over the thumbtack, with the shorter sides facing the top and bottom of the shield. Stick the boss to the shield, then remove the thumbtack.

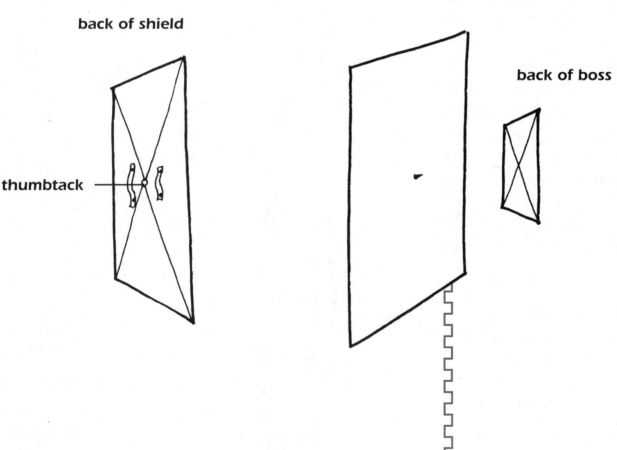

front of shield

back of shield

back of boss

thumbtack

7. Decorate the shield:

a. Cut four strips of yellow construction paper, each 15 x 2 inches (37.5 x 5 cm) long.

b. Put a line of glue on one strip, and press it on the shield diagonally from the corner of the boss to the corner of the shield.

c. Repeat with the other three strips.

8. (Optional) Draw the lightning bolt design shown on the yellow construction paper. Cut it out and glue the strips on the shield as explained in steps 7b and c.

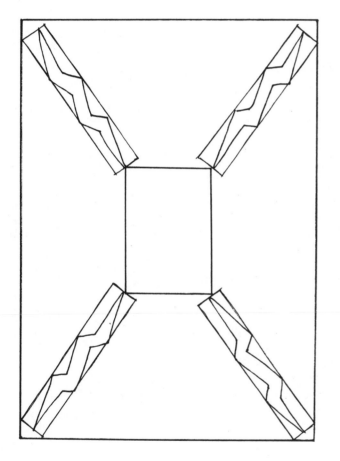

optional lightning bolt

ALL ROADS LEAD TO ROME

Most of the roads built by the legionaries started in the city of Rome. We can still travel on a Roman road called the Via Appia leading out of the city of Rome. The Romans built tombs along their roads so that the dead could enjoy watching travelers pass by. Milestones on the roads marked their distance from the forum in the center of Rome. This led to the famous saying "All roads lead to Rome."

The word "mile" comes from the Latin words "mille passuum," meaning "a thousand paces." The Roman mile equals nine-tenths of a mile (1.4 km).

ACTIVITY

LEGION'S STANDARD

Each of the legions in the Roman army had a sign, called a standard, carried on a pole. The standard was also called an eagle, because there was a statue of an eagle, which stood for the Roman Empire, at the top of every standard. The name of the legion and its motto were shown on a sign below the eagle. In this activity you'll make your own standard.

MATERIALS

4 double sheets of newspaper
masking tape
10-by-24-inch (25-by-60-cm) piece of Con-Tact paper or roll of duct tape
3-by-7-inch (7.5-by-17.5-cm) piece of black poster board
pencil
scissors
4-by-7-inch (10-by-17.5-cm) piece of red poster board
ruler
black marker
glue gun (optional) or white glue
adult helper for glue gun

1. Take the sheets of newspaper by one corner and roll them up tightly, rolling to the opposite corner.

2. Use several pieces of masking tape to fasten the roll together tightly to make a pole.

3. Cover the pole with Con-Tact paper or duct tape.

4. On the black poster board, draw an eagle in pencil. Copy the drawing here or use your own design. Cut out the eagle.

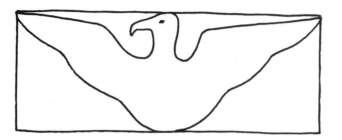

5. On the red poster board, make the sign for the standard by drawing a border in pencil, 1 inch (2.5 cm) in from the edges all around. Go over your line in black marker. Write a Latin name or motto—or both— on the sign and go over it with the marker. See the list of Latin names and sayings in chapter 2.

6. Use white glue or have your adult helper use the glue gun to glue the eagle to the top of the pole. Glue the sign 3 inches (7.5 cm) below the eagle. Now carry your standard proudly!

LEGIONARY'S HELMET

The legionary's helmet was made of iron. For parades, it was decorated with a colorful plume of horsehair dyed red or white. The plume of an ordinary legionary was worn from front to back on his helmet. The officer in charge of a group of one hundred legionaries, who was called a **centurion,** wore the plume from side to side on his helmet. The legionary helmets had brass and copper decoration, like the crown shape you will make for your helmet.

MATERIALS

measuring tape
pencil
5-quart (5-liter) paper paint bucket (from a paint store)
ruler
drawing compass
scissors
roll of duct tape or 24-inch (60-cm) -square piece of Con-Tact paper in gray or brown
2 double sheets of newspaper
9-by-12-inch (23-by-30-cm) sheet of construction paper, either red, white, or black
glue gun (optional) or white glue
10-by-3-inch (25-by-7.5-cm) piece of thin cardboard
adult helper for glue gun and ear flap

1. Make the opening for the face:

a. Turn the bucket upside down on your table. Use the measuring tape and pencil to mark a point on the side of the bucket 3½ inches (8.75 cm) down. Mark this point *A*.

b. Use the tape to measure 2½ inches (6.25 cm) along the side of the bucket from point *A*. Mark this point *C*. Measure 2½ inches (6.25 cm) from point *A* in the other direction. Mark this point *D*. Draw a line connecting points *C* and *D*.

c. Use the ruler to draw a line down from point *A* to the rim. At the rim, mark point *B* at the end of this line. Draw a line connecting points *B* and *C*. Draw another line connecting points *B* and *D*.

d. Use the tape to measure 1½ inches (3.75 cm) along the side of the bucket from point *B*. Mark this point *G*. Measure 1½ inches from point *B* in the other direction. Mark this point *H*. Measure a 2-inch (5-cm) line from point *G* up to line *B–C*. Mark this point *E*. Measure a 2-inch line from point *H* up to line *B–D*. Mark this point *F*.

e. Cut out along the lines *G–E*, *E–C*, *C–D*, *D–F*, and *F–H*.

2. Cut out the ear openings:

a. Put on the bucket with the face opening in front of your face. Ask your helper to use the pencil to draw the outline of your ears on the bucket. Take off the bucket.

b. Cut up from the rim below the ear shapes, and cut out around each ear shape.

3. Make the top of the helmet:

a. Cut four 6-inch (15-cm) strips of duct tape.

b. Crumple the sheets of newspaper into a ball and place the ball on top of the bucket. Use the strips of duct tape to tape the ball of newspaper to the bucket.

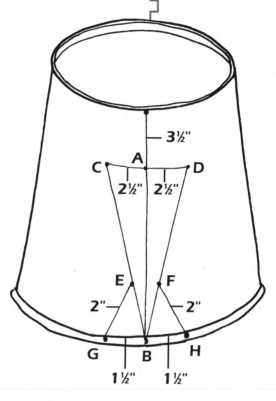

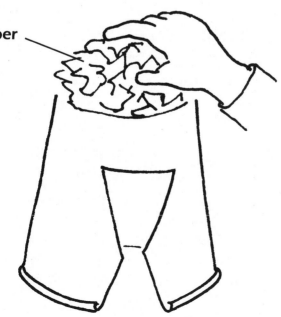

newspaper

4. Cover the helmet:

a. Cut the duct tape in 14-inch (35-cm) strips. If using Con-Tact paper, cut it in strips 4 x 14 inches (10 x 35 cm).

b. Tape these strips on the bucket, from the rim to the top, slightly overlapping them. Continue until the entire bucket and ball of newspaper are covered.

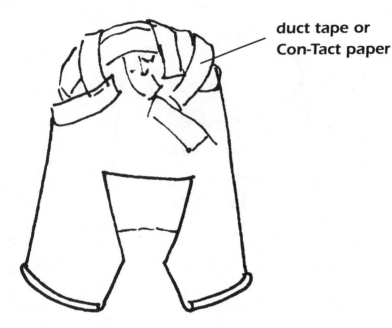

duct tape or Con-Tact paper

5. Make the plume:

a. Fold the sheet of construction paper in half the long way and keep it folded.

b. With the pencil and ruler, draw a line across the folded paper ½ inch (1.25 cm) up from the fold.

c. Keeping the paper folded, make a cut through both halves of the paper from the edges of the paper to the line you drew.

d. Continue to make cuts ½ inch (1.25 cm) apart all along the paper.

e. Fold the paper along the line you drew as shown.

f. Use the white glue or have an adult helper use the glue gun to stick the folded ½-inch (1.25-cm) of paper on the helmet. Glue the strip to the helmet from front to back, starting 5½ inches (14 cm) above the face opening.

fold

6. Make the crown:

a. Find the center point on the strip of thin cardboard by measuring 5 inches (12 cm) from one short end. Draw a vertical line through this point.

b. At each end, mark a point 1 inch (2.5 cm) up from the long side.

c. Draw a curving line connecting these 1-inch (2.5-cm) points to the top of the vertical line. Cut along the curving line.

d. Glue the cardboard lengthwise across the front of the helmet.

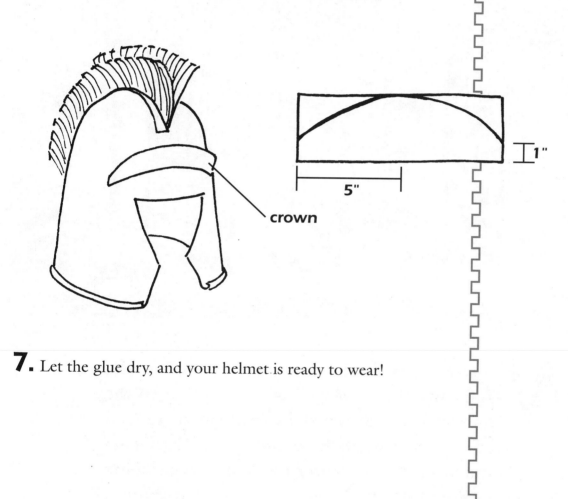

crown

5"

1"

7. Let the glue dry, and your helmet is ready to wear!

CHAPTER·6

JULIA AT THE BATHS

While Marcus is out marching in the parade, Julia and her mother, Livia, are going to the public baths. Servants carry them there in a *litter*, which is like a hammock. Claudia and Calpurnia walk beside the litter. As they enter the high arched doors of the bathhouse, Julia looks around. The bathhouse, built by Emperor *Trajan*, is a splendid building with marble and mosaic walls and floors. It costs so little to use the baths that nearly everyone can afford to come here often. Women and girls use the baths in the morning, and men and boys during the afternoon. Besides hot and cold baths, the bathhouse has massage rooms, indoor and outdoor exercise areas, a library, and a restaurant.

There is even a steam bath, made possible by a Roman invention called a *hypocaust.* This is a furnace in the basement, which sends hot air or steam up through openings in the floor and walls.

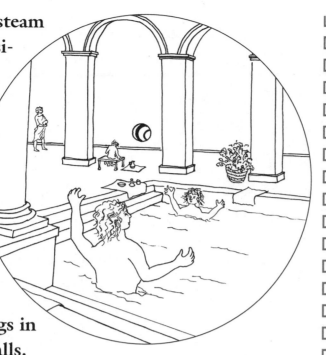

After taking off their clothes, Julia and Livia go to the steam bath to sweat. Then they go to the warm bath, where they play ball in the water. Finally, they cool down by jumping in and out of a cold bath. Calpurnia and Claudia wrap them up in towels, rub scented oil on them, and then clean off the oil with a bronze scraper called a *strigil* (STRIH-jill). Julia goes to the exercise room, where she is delighted to find some of her friends. They lift bronze weights for a while and catch up on all the news of the summer. Her friends tell her she must go to see the new pantomime at the theater. Livia has a massage, talks with friends, and ends by buying a piece of land from her neighbor Domitilla. She sends for Julia to come and write out a contract for the sale. Julia gets a wax tablet and a *stylus* (a pointed stick used for writing) and begins to scratch letters on the tablet.

AQUEDUCTS

Throughout the Roman Empire, water for drinking and bathing in the cities came from mountain lakes and springs. There were no mechanical engines to pump it. The water had to flow on a downhill course, so that the force of gravity would pull it toward the city. To make this possible, the Romans built channels called **aqueducts** (AHK-wuh-dukts). Roman aqueducts look like bridges, and can still be seen in Africa and Europe. In the time this story takes place, nine aqueducts carried over 200 million gallons (758 million liters) of water into Rome every day!

ACTIVITY
WAX TABLET

The Romans wrote notes and messages on wax tablets. These were single or double wooden pads with wax surfaces. The double tablets were called **diptychs** (DIP-ticks), and were joined by hinges so they opened like a book. The Romans wrote on a tablet by scratching the wax surface with a stylus. To erase the writing, they smoothed the wax. They could reuse the tablet as often as they wanted. The tablets were often beautifully decorated and were sometimes covered in ivory. Like the Romans, you can give your writing tablet as a gift!

MATERIALS

pencil
4-by-6-inch (10-by-15-cm) piece of thin cardboard or poster board,
  any color
colored markers
6-by-1½-inch (15-by-3.75-cm) piece of poster board, any color
ruler
scissors
white glue
nonhardening modeling clay (Plasticine or Plastilene or similar)
chopstick or pencil

1. Use the pencil to draw a Roman design like the example here on one side of the 4-by-6-inch (10-by-15-cm) piece of cardboard. If you like, you can include the name of the person who will use it. Remember to use a Roman name and write in capital letters like the Romans!

2. Go over your design with markers.

3. Take the 6-by-1½-inch (15-by-3.75-cm) piece of poster board and draw two lines the long way, each ½ inch (1.25 cm) from the edge. Cut along these lines to get three 6-by-½-inch (15-by-1.25-cm) pieces.

4. Take one of these 6-by-½-inch (15-by-1.25-cm) pieces and cut it in half to get two 3-by-½-inch (7.5-by-1.25-cm) pieces.

5. Take the 4-by-6-inch (10-by-15-cm) piece of cardboard and turn it over so the design is on the back. Glue the small pieces of poster board around the edge as a frame for the tablet as shown in the drawing.

6. Squeeze the modeling clay to make it soft. Press it onto the tablet. Smooth it out to cover the tablet inside the frame with a ¼-inch (0.6-cm) layer of clay.

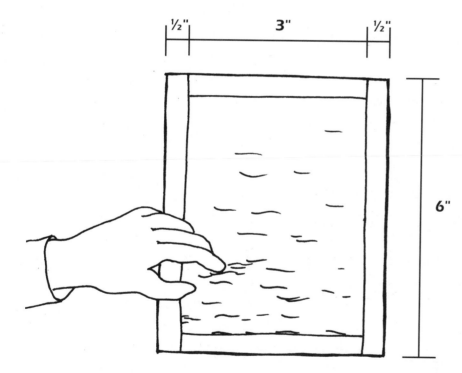

7. Use the chopstick to write a message on your tablet!

ROMAN BUSINESS

Successful Romans were always working at business deals. Many people wanted goods such as spices, silks, jewels, and perfumes from faraway lands. Merchants called importers brought these goods to Rome. They also exported goods made in Rome to other countries. Importing and exporting were risky ways to earn money. Your ship might sink or be attacked. But if successful, you could make a lot of money. Buying and selling land and houses was another way to become rich. Women also worked in these businesses, and many families encouraged their daughters to work in business— even though they still had to obey the paterfamilias.

ACTIVITY

SCROLL

For permanent writing, the Romans used paper made from **papyrus,** a reed that grows in Egypt and southern Italy. They used pen and ink to write on the paper. At the time we are visiting Rome, the Romans had just invented the book, which they called a **codex.** Most people still preferred to write on long strips of paper that were rolled into a scroll. In this activity you'll make your own scroll.

MATERIALS
scissors
large brown paper bag, such as a grocery bag
glue
one-hole paper punch
2-foot (60-cm) length of narrow ribbon
pen

1. Cut out the front of the paper bag. Discard the rest of the bag.

2. Fold the front of the bag in half the long way, with the printed outside folded in.

3. Spread a thin line of glue all over one folded half, on the printed side. Press the other half onto the glue so that it sticks.

4. Punch a hole in the center of one short end of the paper.

5. Fold the ribbon in half and loop it through the hole.

6. Now use the pen to write a message on your scroll. Use capital letters like the Romans!

7. Roll up the scroll. Tie it with the ribbon.

THIS IS A
STORY ABOUT
A ROMAN
GIRL NAM
JULIA

ACTIVITY

ROMAN NUMERALS

We still use the Roman alphabet today—it's our English alphabet. But unlike us, the Romans had no separate system of symbols for numbers. Instead, the Romans used letters to stand for numbers as well as to spell words. We call their numbers Roman numerals. Roman numerals are large and awkward to write, and the Romans had no symbol for zero. But that certainly did not stop the Romans from using math to accomplish amazing feats of engineering!

We still use Roman numbers for chapter headings in some books and for dates on movie credits. Use the Roman Numerals chart and a pencil and some paper—or use your wax tablet and stylus from the "Wax Tablet" activity—and try your hand at some figuring, Roman-style.

Our Arabic Numbers	Roman Numerals
1	I
2	II
3	III
4	IV
5	V
6	VI
7	VII
8	VIII
9	IX
10	X
11	XI
12	XII
13	XIII
14	XIV or XIIII
15	XV
16	XVI
17	XVII
18	XVIII
19	XIX
20	XX
21	XXI
. . .	. . .
30	XXX
40	XL or XXXX
50	L
60	LX
70	LXX
80	LXXX
90	XC or LXXXX
100	C
400	CCCC or CD
500	D
900	CM or DCCCC
1000	M
2000	MM

MATERIALS
Roman Numerals chart
pencil
paper

1. Use the Roman Numerals chart to translate the following dates:

a. MCDXCII   =

b. MDCCLXXVI   =

c. MCMXCVIII   =

d. MMXX   =

2. Add the following Roman numerals:

a. XIX + VII   =

b. XXXIII + V   =

c. LXXI + XII   =

d. CCXI + XLV   =

3. Write these dates using Roman numerals:

a. 753   =

b. 125   =

c. 476   =

d. 27   =

4. Check your answers at the bottom of the page.

Answers

1a. 1492	2a. XXVI	3a. DCCLIII
1b. 1776	2b. XXXVIII	3b. CXXV
1c. 1998	2c. LXXXIII	3c. CDLXXVI
1d. 2020	2d. CCLVI	3d. XXVII

CHAPTER·7

A SPEECH IN THE FORUM

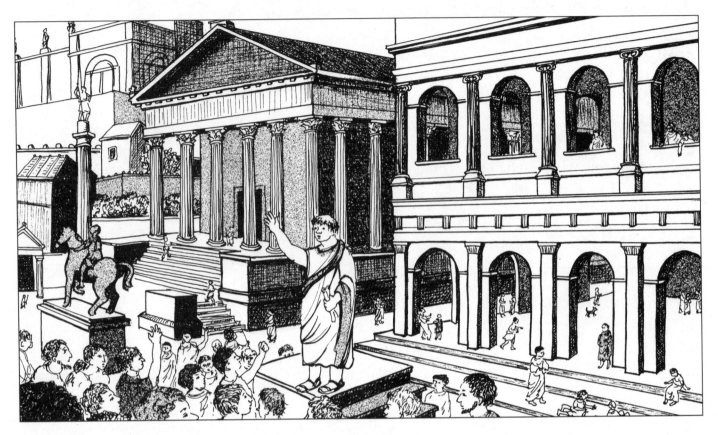

While Marcus is marching, and Julia and Livia are bathing, Senator Julius is at home working in his tablinum. Each day, clients come to the house to ask for Julius's help in legal and political cases. In ancient Rome, there are no professional lawyers. Anyone who wants to argue a law case can do so. Julius is in demand because he is an excellent speaker who can persuade an audience to agree with him. Today a baker asks Julius to speak for him in a law case. He has been accused of burning down a house that he had just sold to an officer in the legions. Julius listens to his story, then agrees to speak for him.

When Marcus comes home after the parade, Julius invites him to go to the law courts in the forum. Marcus is thrilled! He takes off his helmet and grabs his *knuckle-bones,* a game he enjoys, hoping he may have a chance to play with a friend if the debate gets too boring. They set off down the Palatine Hill. Julius's client walks behind them. As they pass the big clock, or sundial, called the *horologium,* it shows the time is just about an hour before noon.

At the forum they enter the courthouse, called the *Basilica Julia.* The crowd grows quiet when Julius begins to speak. Marcus watches the crowd. At first they seem angry at the baker, but as Julius speaks, they calm down.

Julius is able to convince the magistrate, or judge, to let the baker go. The baker is overjoyed. Marcus listens proudly as people congratulate Julius. Julius puts his arm around Marcus's shoulders. He asks if he would like to go to see the gladiatorial games, contests where men called *gladiators* fight one another. Marcus skips along happily. He can't wait to go to the *Colosseum,* the huge stone *amphitheater,* or arena, where the gladiatorial games are held. He has forgotten all about missing Tibur—there are no gladiators there!

In ancient Rome, the purpose of higher education was to produce successful citizens. Citizens needed to be able to take part in all areas of life. Many young men joined the legions and became soldiers for a few years. Then they became merchants for a few more years and made money trading. They might make a name for themselves by arguing law cases. Then, when they were older, they became politicians. At all stages of life, Romans needed to be able to argue their point of view and persuade other people that their side was right. This art is still known as rhetoric.

ACTIVITY

KNUCKLEBONES

For thousands of years people have used sheep's knucklebones to try to tell the future. They have also played games with them. Some Roman paintings and mosaics show women and children playing knucklebones. Soldiers in the Roman legions enjoyed playing knucklebones, too, and spread the game wherever they went. Make five clay knucklebones and play a game with your friends.

MATERIALS

1 cup (250 ml) white glue
1 cup (250 ml) water
bowl
plastic spoon
2 paper towels
ruler
glass or ceramic plate
2 to 4 players

1. To make the knucklebones:
a. Pour the glue and the water into the bowl. Stir with the spoon to mix them together.
b. Tear the paper towels into small pieces, about 1 x 2 inches (2.5 x 5 cm) each.
c. Put the paper bits into the bowl and stir well, so that the paper absorbs all the glue mixture.
d. Take some of the paper out of the bowl and press it in your hands into a 1-inch (2.5-cm) cube. Press the piece tightly. Squeeze the sides in so it is pinched in the middle, as in the drawing.

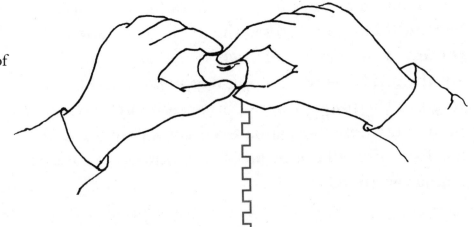

e. Repeat step 1d to make four more knucklebones.

f. Put the knucklebones on the plate. Let them dry for 24 hours.

2. Knucklebones is played like jacks. The players throw the bones up in the air. They must catch them in special ways. Here is a popular version of the game (2 to 4 players):

a. The first player throws the five bones into the air. Then he tries to catch all of them on the back of his hand.

b. However many he catches, he throws them up again and tries to catch them in the palm of his hand. His score is the number of bones he holds in his palm.

c. Each player does this in turn. The player with the highest score is the winner.

Marcus likes to play with several other toys besides his knucklebones. He is getting too old to play with his toy horses and chariots, but he still enjoys rolling a hoop and tossing dice with his friends. His dice are made of bone. Marcus also likes to spend a lot of time with his horses and dogs.

Julia is much more interested in jewelry and clothes than in toys. She would much prefer to meet her friends at the bathhouse than stay home

ROMAN EDUCATION

As a young boy or girl in Rome you went to school to learn reading, writing, arithmetic, history, and poetry from a **litterator.** If you were a girl, by age twelve you were through with school, and were learning how to care for a home and family from your mother. If she had a trade, she taught it to you also. Roman women had many trades, including baking, hairdressing, laundry, and medicine. At age eleven, if you were a boy, you moved up a class to study Greek from a **grammaticus.** By fourteen, most boys left school and went to work. Marcus and some other boys would go on to higher education with a **rhetor,** who taught them law, politics, and how to speak in public. A few lucky boys ended their education by going away to study with the best teachers, in Athens.

and play with her beautiful dolls. When Julia stopped playing with them, Claudia wrapped her dolls up and put them carefully away, saying they should be kept for Julia's daughters!

ACTIVITY

HOROLOGIUM

A sundial consists of a pointer, called a **gnomon** (NO-mon), and a flat surface, which is the dial. The hours of the day are marked on the dial. The gnomon's shadow on the dial points to the time of day. The emperor Augustus set up a huge sundial in the Campus Martius (CAMP-oos MAR-tee-oos), or Field of Mars, on the edge of the city of Rome. This sundial was called the Solarium Augustii (so-LAHR-ee-oom ow-GOOS-tee-ee) (Augustus's sundial), or the Horologium (clock). The hours were marked out on the ground. The pointer was a tall **obelisk,** or pointed column built as a memorial, brought back from Egypt.

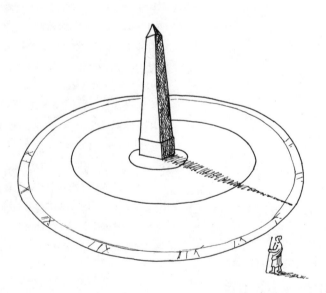

You can make a small sundial to tell the hours. You may want to write a motto on your sundial. Choose from the Latin mottoes on page 65.

LATIN MOTTOES

Tempus fugit.	Time flies.
Carpe diem.	Seize the day.
Ecce hora (EK-kay HO-rah).	Now is the hour.
Festina lente.	Make haste slowly.
Lux post umbram.	Light after shadow.
Non sine lumine.	Nothing without light.
Sol splendit omnibus.	The sun shines on everyone.

MATERIALS

pencil

ruler

*8-inch (20-cm) square of foam board (from a crafts supply store)
   or corrugated cardboard*

drawing compass

scissors

5-by-3-inch (12.5-by-7.5-cm) piece of corrugated cardboard

white glue

black marker

Latin Mottoes list

1. Use the pencil and ruler to draw a diagonal line from corner to corner on the foam board square. Draw another diagonal line between the other corners. The point where the diagonal lines cross is the center point.

2. Place the drawing compass on the center point. Use the pencil and compass to draw an 8-inch (20-cm) circle on the foam board. Cut out the circle. This will be the dial.

3. Measure in 1 inch (2.5 cm) from the bottom left corner on the long side of the 5-by-3-inch (12.5-by-7.5-cm) piece of corrugated cardboard. Mark this point X.

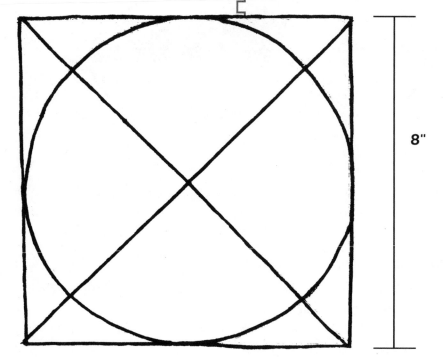

8"

4. Mark point Y at the top left corner of the cardboard rectangle, as shown in the diagram. Use the pencil and ruler to draw a line from point X to point Y.

5. Mark point Z at the bottom right corner, opposite point Y, as shown. Use the ruler and pencil to draw a line from point Y to point Z.

6. Cut along lines XY and YZ. This triangle is the gnomon.

5"

Y

3"

X

1"

Z

7. Put a line of glue along the bottom of the gnomon (from point X to point Z).

8. Stand the gnomon on the circle, with point X at the center of the circle and point Z on the edge of the circle. Press the gnomon down so it will stick, and hold it until the glue dries.

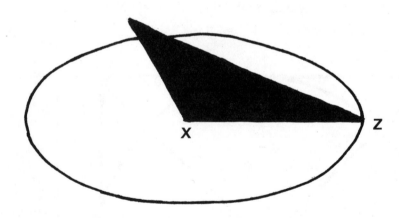

X Z

9. Use the black marker to write a motto from the Latin Mottoes list around the edge of the circle.

10. Take your sundial outdoors at noon on a sunny day. Use a pencil to write XII (12) where the gnomon's shadow falls on the edge of the circle.

11. Leave the dial outside. Go back at 3:00 P.M., 6:00 P.M., and 9:00 P.M. At each time, write III (3), VI (6), or IX (9) where the shadow falls on the edge of the circle.

12. Go over the Roman numerals in black marker. Test your sundial on another sunny day to see if it tells the same time!

ROMAN HOURS

A Roman hour was different from our sixty-minute hour. In ancient Rome the length of an hour changed during different seasons. The Roman hour was one-twelfth of the hours of daylight. Since daylight lasts much longer in summer than in winter, the Roman hour was about ninety minutes in summer and about forty-five minutes in winter.

CHAPTER 8

GAMES OF THE GLADIATORS

At noon, after a walk across Rome, Marcus, Julius, and Jason arrive at the Colosseum. The Colosseum is an oval arena that can hold fifty thousand people. It was built for the people by Emperor *Vespasian* (ves-PAY-zhun) (A.D. 9–79, reigned 70–79). It was named for the giant statue called the Colossus, which stood near the arena. Marcus looks up at the Colosseum as they climb up the stone steps. The walls are made from three rows of big stone arches, built one on top of the other. Many stairs and passages make it easy for everyone in the audience to get to their seats.

Julius leads them up to seats near the emperor's box. The emperor is not there, but another senator, called Honorius, is in charge of the games. Honorius welcomes Julius and Marcus. They sit beside

Honorius on cushioned marble seats. The Colosseum has no roof, but a big sunshade is pulled out to keep the sun off the better seats. Jason buys bread, cheese, grapes, and cool water from a stall for their lunch. Marcus is hungry and enjoys it all.

The gladiatorial games are fights between gladiators, or between gladiators and wild animals. Most gladiators are slaves, or prisoners who have been captured in a war. In the morning games at the Colosseum, wild animals fight other animals, or gladiators or prisoners. Thousands of animals, including elephants and panthers, are killed at each show. Marcus prefers the afternoon games, in which the gladiators fight one another.

It is very noisy, with musicians playing, gladiators fighting, and the crowd cheering for their favorites and jeering at the losers. Marcus watches a fight between a gladiator with a spear and a net, and another gladiator with a short sword and a round shield. Marcus cheers when the swordsman knocks the other gladiator to the ground. Senator Honorius gives the thumbs-up sign, which means that the losing gladiator's life will be spared because he fought bravely.

GLADIATORIAL GAMES

The gladiator games began centuries before the Roman Empire, among the Etruscan people of northern Italy. When the Etruscans buried an important person, they had his slaves fight and kill one another during the funeral. Then the slaves were buried with their master.

The Romans believed that these fights were pleasing to the gods. The Romans held gladiatorial games on religious festivals. The Romans also used the games as a way of executing condemned criminals, who were forced to fight each other or wild animals.

Marcus knows that the penalty for losing a gladiatorial fight is often death. As part of the audience at the games, he helps to decide whether or not the losing gladiator should be killed. When a gladiator is knocked down by his opponent, the official in charge of the games looks to the crowd for a decision. If they thought the losing gladiator had fought bravely, they cheered him. If they thought he had fought in a cowardly way, they booed.

The official then holds out his hand and gives the thumbs-up or thumbs-down sign. Thumbs-up meant the winner should spare the loser's life. Thumbs-down meant the winner should kill the loser. The winning gladiator is given a bag of coins for his prize. He will have to come back later to fight again, until he wins enough money to buy his freedom.

ACTIVITY

ROMAN BUILDINGS

You can find buildings modeled after the ancient Roman style everywhere. Government buildings, colleges, churches, and other important public structures are often built in Roman style. Play a game to see how many Roman-style buildings you can find!

MATERIALS
city or town center
pencil
pad of paper
Roman-Style Buildings pictures
2 or more players

1. Next time you are in a city or town, see how many Roman-style buildings you can find.

— dome

2. Each player gets one point for each building found. Keep track of the points with the pencil and paper. The player with the most points wins.

3. To recognize a Roman-style building, look for features shown in the Roman-Style Buildings pictures:

a. *Arches.* Roman-style buildings have round arches in porches and over windows and doors. They may also have round arches inside the building over stairs and hallways.

b. *Domes.* The middle of the roof of a Roman-style building is often topped with a big round dome. Domes are sometimes covered in gold.

c. *Columns.* These are pillars, usually built across the front of the building, that support the roof.

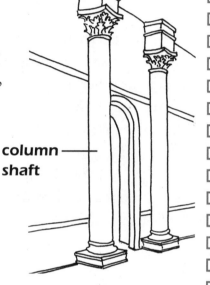

column shaft

column capital

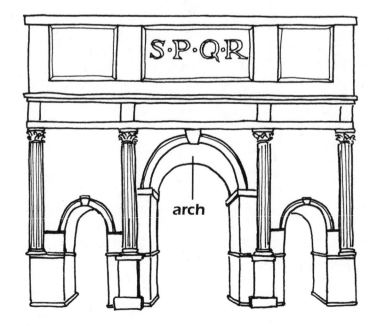

S·P·Q·R

arch

The ancient Romans were excellent builders. Many of their buildings still stand, and they have been copied countless times in countries all over the world. Ancient Roman buildings were huge; they had round arches over their doors and windows, and round domes on top of their roofs. The Romans developed **concrete**, a mixture of stones set in cement, and used it for roads and large buildings. The walls of their public buildings were usually made of concrete covered in brick or marble.

Pillars called columns are often built across the front of Roman-style buildings. A Roman-style column usually has a fancy capital, which is the top part of the column on which the roof rests. The long body of the column is the **shaft.** A Roman-style column may have a plain, smooth shaft, or the shaft may be fluted with ridges running up the sides.

TRIUMPHAL ARCH PLAQUE

When a Roman emperor or a general defeated a foreign army, the Roman people celebrated with a big parade through Rome. The Roman soldiers marched with all the captives they had taken—men, women, and children, and everything else they had seized—animals, jewels, money, and other valuables. The parade marched through a triumphal arch, an arch built over a street to honor the armies, on which the names of the legions and their battles were carved in stone. Many other cities have built similar arches since.

The Romans wrote SPQR on their monuments. These letters stood for *Senatus Populusque Romanus* (The Senate and People of Rome). The letters showed that the arch or other monument was erected on behalf of all the people. You may want to write these letters after your name on the plaque you make in this activity.

To write your name on your plaque's arch, end your name in *-i* if you are a boy or in *-ae* if you are a girl. For example, write ARCUS MARCI (ARK-oos MARK-ee) for "Marcus's Arch" or ARCUS JULIAE (ARK-oos YOOL-ee-eye) for "Julia's Arch." (The Latin word for arch is *arcus.*)

MATERIALS

several sheets of newspaper
one-hole paper punch
ruler
6-by-7-inch (15-by-17.5-cm) piece of thin cardboard
1 pound (0.5 kg) self-hardening clay
resealable plastic bag
two 8-by-9-inch (20-by-23-cm) pieces of waxed paper
rolling pin
craft stick or modeling tool
pencil
12-inch (30-cm) length of ribbon or string

1. Spread some of the newspaper over your work surface.

2. Use the paper punch to make a hole in the two top corners of the cardboard, ½ inch (1.25 cm) in from the top and sides.

3. Divide the clay in half. Place one half in the plastic bag and seal the bag.

4. Take the remaining piece of clay and mold it in your hands until it is warm and feels soft. Place it on one piece of waxed paper, and cover it with the other piece.

5. Use the rolling pin to roll the clay out flat until it is the same size as the cardboard, about 6 x 7 inches (15 x 17.5 cm), and about ¼ inch (0.6 cm) thick. Pull off the top piece of waxed paper and set it aside.

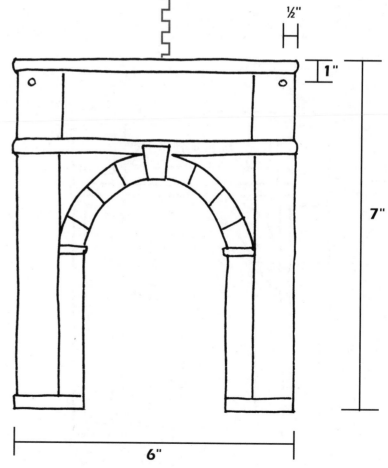

6. Turn the clay over and press it onto the cardboard until it sticks. Pull off the other piece of waxed paper and set it aside. Use the craft stick to trim off the excess clay around the edges. The clay-covered cardboard will be your plaque.

7. Use the pencil to draw the outline of the arch as shown on the clay. Use the pencil to scratch the surface of the clay inside the outline to make it slightly rough.

8. Take the second piece of clay out of the plastic bag and repeat steps 4 and 5.

9. Use the pencil to draw the parts of the arch as shown in the picture on the second piece of clay. Press the pencil into the clay to cut around each part.

10. Lift off the parts, one at a time, and press them in place on your plaque. Smooth the clay with your fingers or the craft stick.

11. Use the pencil and craft stick to draw a design and write an inscription on your arch. Write your Roman name on the arch.

12. Find the holes you punched at the top corners of the cardboard in step 2. Use the pencil to poke out the holes from the front to the back of the clay.

13. Put your plaque on a clean sheet of newspaper. Let it dry for 2 days away from sunny windows, radiators, or other sources of heat.

14. When the clay is dry, thread the ribbon through the holes. Tie a knot in the ribbon. Now hang up your plaque.

ACTIVITY

TRIUMPHAL COLUMN

Some Roman emperors were not satisfied to celebrate their battles by just raising arches. They also built huge columns that towered high in the air. The emperor Trajan built a triumphal column in Rome that still stands today. Figures carved around it show Emperor Trajan winning a war. There is a figure of Trajan in armor on top of the column, like the figure on the top of your column.

MATERIALS

black marker
paper towel roll
pencil
ruler
empty single-serving cereal box (from a multipack)
scissors
5-inch (12.5-cm) piece of duct tape
12-by-6-inch (30-by-15-cm) piece of gray or black Con-Tact paper
*   *or construction paper*
white glue
2½-inch (6.25 cm) -square piece of corrugated cardboard
small plastic figure of a Roman soldier (or other small
*   figure), about 2 inches (5 cm) tall*

1. Use the marker to draw a spiral line up the towel roll, following the seam of the roll. Draw a pencil line around the roll 1½ inches (3.75 cm) in from one end. This end will be the bottom.

2. Starting at the pencil line, draw a picture all the way up one side of the towel roll, staying within the spiral lines. Draw something you are proud of, such as a game you won or something you did.

3. Use the pencil and ruler to draw a diagonal line from corner to corner on the front of the cereal box. Draw another diagonal line between the other corners. The point where the diagonal lines cross is the center.

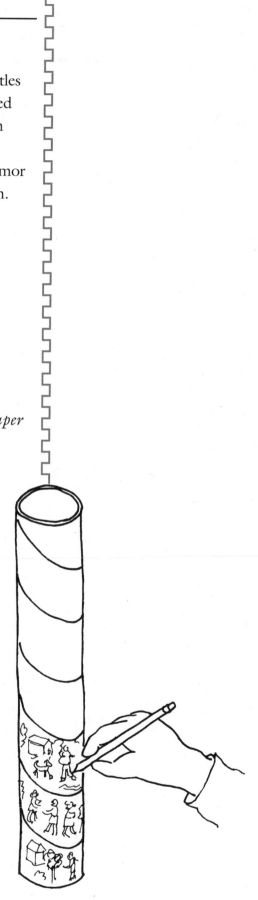

4. Lay the box on its back and stand the towel roll on the center point of the front of the box. Draw a line on the box around the bottom of the roll. Cut out this circle.

5. Push the towel roll all the way into the box through the circle you have cut out. Cut the duct tape into three pieces. Use the duct tape to fasten the roll and box together.

6. Cut out two pieces of Con-Tact paper, each 4 x 3 inches (10 x 7.5 cm). Stick the paper (or glue it, if using construction paper) to the top (front) of the cereal box, starting at the towel roll and wrapping the paper around the sides of the box.

7. Cut out two more pieces of Con-Tact paper, 1½ x 3 inches (3.75 x 7.5 cm) each. Stick the paper pieces on the ends of the cereal box. Cut small pieces of Con-Tact paper to stick over any other bits of the cereal box that are showing.

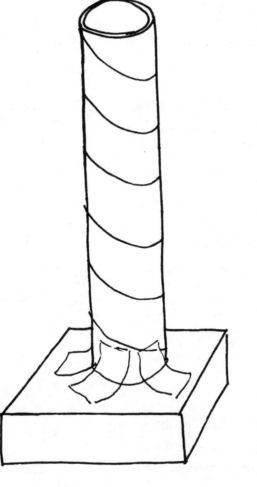

8. Cut a 3-inch (7.5-cm) square of Con-Tact paper. Stick it on the top and sides of the square of corrugated cardboard.

9. Cut a 2½-inch (6.25-cm) square of Con-Tact paper. Stick it on the bottom of the cardboard square.

10. Use the glue to fasten the Roman soldier to the top of the cardboard square.

11. Put glue on the bottom of the cardboard square and fasten it to the top of the towel roll. Let it dry, and your column is finished!

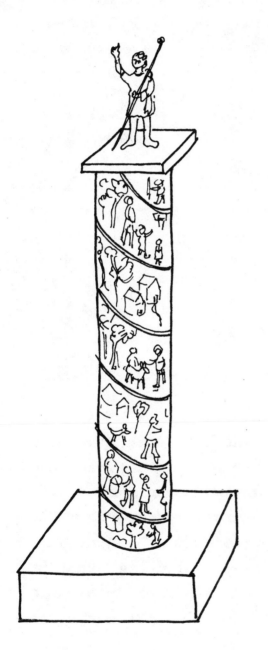

CHAPTER 9

AT THE THEATER

Back home after visiting the bathhouse, Julia and Livia have a light lunch before getting ready for the theater. This afternoon they are going to see the new *pantomime*, a stage performance in which the actors don't talk, but present a story about Roman gods and goddesses through singing and dancing. Claudia arranges Julia's hair in a knot on her neck, and brings out her jewelry box. Julia selects her favorite earrings. Calpurnia piles up Livia's hair under a beautiful gold headpiece called a tiara. Livia is also wearing a gold necklace and bracelet.

Four attendants carry Livia and Julia in a litter. They go down several streets toward the river to reach the theater, where the pantomime is held. The theater is a big stone building with stone benches for forty thousand people. Livia and Julia sit on marble chairs near the stage.

Musicians play, the curtain is lowered to reveal the stage, and the pantomime begins. The actors and actresses wear wonderful costumes and masks that show the personalities of their characters. Julia enjoys the pantomime just as much as her friends at the bathhouse had told her she would. She claps heartily at the end.

ACTIVITY

PANTOMIME MASK

Roman actors and actresses wore masks over their faces to show the characters they played. Sometimes an actor wore two masks at the same time, one over the face and one on the back of the head. By quickly switching masks, an actor could play two different characters in the same play, or show two different emotions or two sides of a single character.

A pantomime actor did not speak, so the mask did not have an opening for the mouth. Make your own actor's mask from a paper plate. If you choose to make two masks, do this activity twice. Make each of the masks with a different face. Tie the two masks together loosely so you can wear one on your face and one on the back of your head as you put on your own pantomime.

MATERIALS

9-inch (23-cm) paper plate
pencil
ruler
scissors
fine-point marker, black or other dark color
one-hole paper punch
6-foot (2-m) length of black or brown yarn or ribbon (optional)
2-foot (60-cm) length of string or yarn

1. On the front of the plate, use the pencil to draw two small round eyes, each approximately ½ inch (1.25 cm) across.

2. Draw a large mouth, approximately 2 inches (5 cm) across and ¾ inch (2 cm) high. Curve the mouth down for a sad face, up for a happy face.

3. Use the scissors to cut out the eyes.

4. Draw a nose about 2 inches (5 cm) long.

5. With the marker, draw around the eyes, mouth, and nose. Draw in the hair around the top and sides of the mask. Draw eyebrows, ears, and any other features you choose.

6. (Optional) Make a beard:
a. Starting directly below the mouth, punch a hole ¼ inch (0.6 cm) in from the edge of the mask.
b. Punch a second hole ¼ inch to the right of the first hole.
c. Punch seven more holes ¼ inch apart along the lower right side.
d. Punch eight holes ¼ inch apart along the lower left side of the mask.
e. Cut the 6-foot length of yarn into 17 pieces, each 4 inches (10 cm) long.
f. Tie one piece of yarn through each hole, knotting the yarn in front of the mask as shown on page 81.

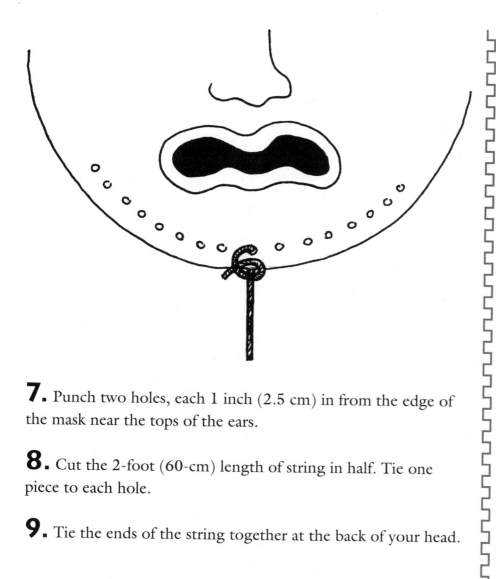

7. Punch two holes, each 1 inch (2.5 cm) in from the edge of the mask near the tops of the ears.

8. Cut the 2-foot (60-cm) length of string in half. Tie one piece to each hole.

9. Tie the ends of the string together at the back of your head.

ACTIVITY

TIARA

For special occasions, Roman women wore their hair arranged on top of their heads in fancy curls. When they dined or went out, they loved to wear lots of jewelry. They often wore gold tiaras with many gems. Make your own tiara and wear it for dress-up!

MATERIALS

24-by-1-inch (60-by-2.5-cm) strip of dark blue or black poster board

stapler

fifteen 12-inch (30-cm) -long metallic-gold pipe cleaners (from a crafts supply store)

Many Romans enjoyed going to the theater. At the theater, they could choose between a concert, a play, or a pantomime with music and dancing. In the serious plays, male actors played the parts of both men and women. But in the pantomimes, both women and men acted, dressed in wonderful costumes and with realistic sets.

Most Roman theaters had no roofs, but were built like arenas, with rows of stone seats rising up around the walls. At the back of the stage there was a stage house. This was three stories high, with many doors through which the actors came and went. The actors used the upper floors of the stage house for special effects, such as the arrival of gods and goddesses. Roman engineers placed big empty jars all around the theater to make the sound louder. So no matter how far back you were sitting, you could hear the music and songs.

ruler

5 golden buttons decorated with fake gems, or any colorful buttons, all the same or different (from a crafts supply store)

5 paper clips, gold-colored if available

helper

1. Have your helper hold the strip of poster board around your head. The helper should overlap the ends until the tiara fits. Staple the ends together.

2. Fold over about ½ inch (1.25 cm) of a pipe cleaner on the inside lower edge of the tiara. Wrap the pipe cleaner up over the outside of the tiara and down over the inside again. Wrap the pipe cleaner around the tiara again two times.

3. Wrap the pipe cleaner around the tiara another time, but this time extend it above the top of the tiara ½ inch (1.25 cm). Wrap the pipe cleaner around the tiara again.

4. Twist the ½-inch (1.25-cm) end of the pipe cleaner that extends above the tiara.

5. Repeat steps 2–4 with the other pipe cleaners.

6. Thread a button on a paper clip. Fasten the clip on the tiara, with the button on the outside.

7. Repeat step 6 with the other buttons, spacing them evenly around the front of the tiara.

ACTIVITY
NECKLACE

Roman ladies wore necklaces made of several strands of gold braided together. You can ornament your necklace with golden buttons decorated with fake pearls or gems.

MATERIALS

scissors

yardstick (meterstick)

7½-foot (2.5-m) length of golden or yellow thin cord (from a crafts supply store)

ruler

9 assorted golden buttons decorated with fake pearls or gems, or any colorful buttons

golden or yellow paper clip (If golden or yellow is not available, use a regular paper clip.)

1. Use the scissors to cut three lengths of cord, each 24 inches (60 cm) long. Set the rest of the cord aside.

2. Tie the ends of the three pieces of cord together at one end.

3. Braid the strips and tie them together at the other end.

4. Take the cord you set aside in step 1. Cut it into nine pieces, each 2 inches (5 cm) long.

5. Thread a 2-inch (5-cm) piece of cord through a button.

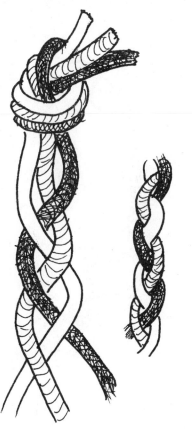

6. Find the center front of the braided cord. Push one end of the 2-inch (5-cm) cord from step 5 through the center of the braid. Tie the ends of the cord together so that the button is fastened tightly to the braid.

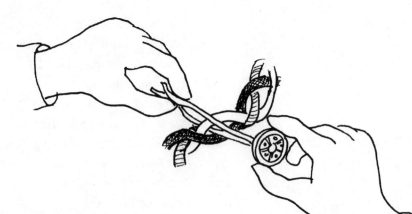

7. Repeat steps 5 and 6 to tie the other eight buttons to the braid. Space the buttons 2 inches (5 cm) apart.

8. Push the paper clip through one end of the braid. Use the clip to fasten the necklace together.

ACTIVITY

BRACELET

The Romans loved color. Sometimes they wore jewelry made of large pieces of gold coated with enamel, which is colored glass baked on metal. You can make a colorful bracelet of your own. Measure your bracelet to make it the right size for your wrist.

MATERIALS

scissors
5-by-1¼-inch (12.5-by-3-cm) strip of dark blue or red
*   poster board*
ruler
1-yard (1-m) length of golden or yellow cord (from a crafts
*   supply store)*
glue gun (optional) or white glue
4 glass gems with one flat side (from a crafts supply store)
golden or yellow paper clip (If golden or yellow is not available,
*   use a regular paper clip.)*
adult helper for glue gun

1. Use the scissors to cut the poster board strip into four squares, each 1¼ x 1¼ inches (3 x 3 cm).

2. Use the scissors to cut two 10-inch (25-cm) pieces of cord. Set the rest of the cord aside.

3. Place the four cardboard squares on a table, ¼ inch (0.6 cm) apart. Lay the two cords side by side across the middle of the cardboard squares, ¼ inch (0.6 cm) apart.

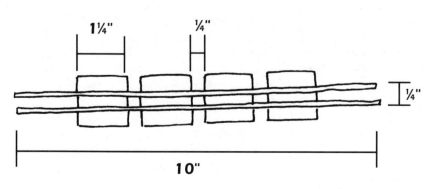

4. Use white glue or have your adult helper use the glue gun to stick the cords to the cardboard squares.

5. Let the glue dry, then tie the ends of the cords together in a double knot, about ½ inch (1.25 cm) from the end squares. Bend the loose end of each cord back over the knot and glue the end to the closest cardboard square.

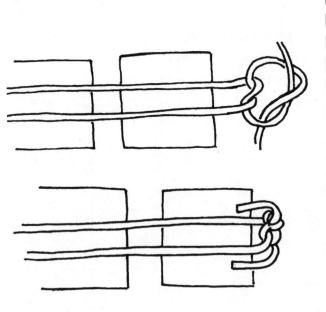

6. Turn the bracelet over. Use white glue or have your adult helper use the glue gun to stick a glass gem to the middle of each cardboard square.

7. Cut the remaining cord in half, and then in half again.

8. Use white glue or have your adult helper use the glue gun to stick a piece of cord around each gem, ⅛ inch (0.3 cm) from the edge of the cardboard square. Press the cord down.

9. Hook the paper clip through one end loop of cord. Use it to fasten the bracelet together.

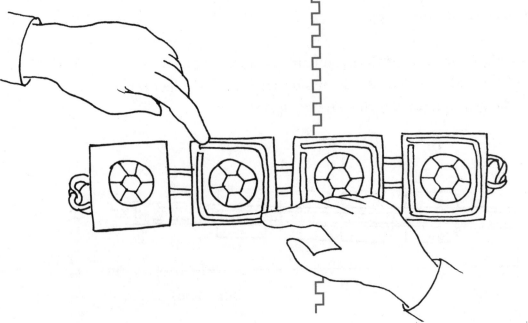

CHAPTER·10

AT THE CIRCUS

While Julius and Marcus are watching the games at the Colosseum, Tullius arrives with a message. Julius reads it, and tells Marcus their friend Marcellus has invited them to join him at the Circus Maximus. Marcus is delighted! They say good-bye to Senator Honorius and walk through the forum to the Circus.

The Circus Maximus, or Biggest Circus, is the chariot-racing arena in Rome. It is the most popular place in Rome for entertainment. More than two hundred thousand people can fit in the Circus. On this festival day the Circus is crowded. Julius and Marcus join Marcellus in seats near the starting gate, where four chariots are lined up.

Each chariot is drawn by four horses, which snort and paw with excitement. The chariots are made of wood or wicker. They are light, so the horses can run fast while pulling them. The chariot drivers wear tunics in the color of their teams: the Reds, the Whites, the Blues, and the Greens. Marcus wants the Blue team to win! All around them, people are taking out coins to bet on the winner.

A napkin is thrown onto the track. This is the signal to start, and the horses are off in a cloud of dust! Marcus coughs. He turns around and sees soldiers wearing plumed helmets marching toward them. It is the Praetorian (pree-TOR-ee-un) Guard, the emperor's own bodyguards! And there is Emperor Hadrian himself, walking up to his box to watch the races. He stops to greet Senator Julius, and then invites the family to join him for dinner this evening. Marcus is amazed—he has never been to the palace before. What a great evening this will be! He is so excited he hardly notices when the Blue chariot wins, and the chariot driver steps up to receive his gold winner's wreath and a big bag of coins.

Marcus knows that long ago Rome was not an empire, a state governed by an emperor. His litterator teaches him that for five hundred years Rome was a republic, a state in which the people elected their leaders. Then in 46 B.C. the Romans elected their leader, Julius Caesar, dictator for life. When Julius Caesar died in 44 B.C. the Romans elected his great-nephew Octavian (63 B.C.–A.D. 14) emperor, with the title Augustus. Before he died, Octavian appointed his stepson Tiberius (42 B.C.–A.D. 37) as the next emperor.

For five hundred years Rome remained an empire, with each emperor choosing the next emperor, until Rome's defeat in 476. But even when an emperor ruled, senators, consuls, magistrates, and other Roman officials still had considerable political power. The emperor chose senators to be the governors of provinces and leaders of the army.

ACTIVITY

WINNER'S WREATH

The Romans awarded their best athletes wreaths made of bronze covered in gold, forged in the shape of leaves. Men often wore these gold wreaths at dinner parties. Your wreath will look like a Roman winner's wreath!

MATERIALS
several sheets of newspaper
pencil
ruler
1-by-22½-inch (2.5-by-56.25-cm) strip of cardboard in any color
scissors
one-hole paper punch
18-inch (45-cm) length of narrow ribbon in any color

BREAD AND CIRCUSES

Roman emperors were afraid that unemployed people would riot or steal. To keep the people happy, the government gave them free wheat to make bread. The emperor and senators also paid for free entertainment for everyone. They put on plays in the theaters, gladiatorial games in the Colosseum, and chariot races in the Circus Maximus. The Romans called this policy of free bread and free entertainment **Panis et Circenses** (Bread and Circuses).

*fourteen 3- to 4-inch (7.5- to 10-cm) -long pieces of imitation
    leafy plants such as ivy (from a crafts supply store)*
paintbrush
gold paint

1. Spread the newspaper over your work area.

2. Use the pencil and ruler to draw lines down the middle of
the cardboard strip. Start 1 inch (2.5 cm) in from one end. Draw
a 1-inch (2.5-cm) -long line. Leave a ½-inch (1.25-cm) space,
then draw a second 1-inch (2.5-cm) -long line. Continue skip-
ping spaces and drawing lines to the end of the strip as shown.

3. Use the scissors to cut through each of the 1-inch (2.5-cm)
lines. If you find it hard to start each cut, use the paper punch to
make a starter hole.

4. Punch a hole at each end of the cardboard strip, ½ inch
(1.25 cm) in from the ends.

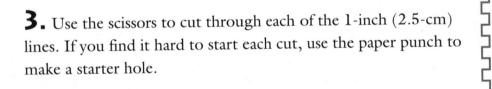

5. Tie the ribbon loosely through the punched holes and try your wreath on for size. If it is too large, move one end of the ribbon to one of the slits you cut in step 2, and cut off the extra cardboard. If it is too small, extend the ribbon and leave some space between the ends of the cardboard.

6. When the size is right, take off the wreath and tie the ribbon in a bow.

7. Push one end of the short pieces of your plants through each slit in the cardboard. Pull them through firmly so that they won't fall out when you wear the wreath.

8. Use the brush to paint the leaves gold. When the paint has dried, wear your golden wreath with the toga you made in chapter 4!

ACTIVITY
COINS

The Romans minted coins of gold, silver, brass, and copper. They had no paper money. The most valuable coin was the gold *aureus*. The least valuable was the copper *quadrans*. The Roman emperors issued coins with their pictures on one side. On the other side, they might show something of which they were proud. For example, Emperor Vespasian's picture was on one side of his coins, and on the other was a picture of the Colosseum, which he built.

In this activity, imagine that you are the emperor making your own coin. Before you begin, think about how you want to design it. On one side you will show a picture of your head in profile (turned to the side) and your Roman name. What do you want to show on the other side? A game you won? A project or activity you did that makes you proud?

ROMAN COINS

Coin	Metal	Value
aureus	gold	25 denarii
denarius	silver	4 sesterces
sestertius (ses-TER-tee-oos)	brass	2½ asses
as	copper	4 quadrans
quadrans	copper	¼ as

MATERIALS

bottle caps in several sizes
cardboard scraps
pencil
scissors
black fine-point marker

1. Put a bottle cap on the cardboard and draw around it in pencil.

2. Cut out the circle. This will be your coin.

3. Use the pencil to draw your profile and write your Roman name on one side. Draw your special event or project on the other.

4. Go over your drawings and name with the marker.

5. Repeat steps 1–4 using different-size bottle caps to make different-size coins. Try different designs. Make as many coins as you want!

CHAPTER·11

THE EMPEROR'S FEAST

After Marcus and his father return from the chariot race, and Julia and her mother return from
the theater, Julius tells Livia that Emperor
Hadrian has invited the whole family to dinner. Julia and
Marcus are delighted. They admire Emperor Hadrian,
and know that they are lucky that he is their emperor.

They have read stories about Emperor Nero (A.D.
37–68, reigned 54–68), for example. Nero was a wicked
man and a terrible emperor. He murdered his mother, his
wife, and his stepbrother. A legend tells that while a
dreadful fire destroyed half of Rome, Nero did nothing to
help, but sat playing a stringed musical instrument called
a lyre—he thought of himself as a musician and a poet.

But as well as emperors like Nero and Caligula (reigned 37–41), there were good emperors like Augustus, Trajan, Hadrian, and Marcus Aurelius (reigned 161–180), who ruled fairly, kept the empire strong and generally peaceful, and made life better for the people by giving them jobs and building handsome temples, theaters, arenas, and baths.

Julia and Marcus hurry to change into their best clothes. As Claudia arranges Julia's hair, she reminds her to watch her manners at dinner. Finally, they are all ready. Servants with torches light their way on the short journey to the Palatine Hill, where the emperor lives in his palace ("palace" comes from "Palatine"). At the palace, a soldier of the Praetorian Guard leads them to the triclinium, where dinner will be served. Lights from many oil lamps and torches make the atrium as bright as noon, and incense perfumes the air. Julia is trying to look at everything, and at the same time not to seem curious. She has never seen so many well-dressed people. All the men wear gold wreaths. All the women are covered in jewelry.

Everyone stands up as the emperor and his party enter. Emperor Hadrian greets his guests, who reply *"Ave!"* which means "Hail!" Before they begin to eat, Emperor Hadrian throws a salt cake into the fire to honor the goddess Vesta. The chief Vestal Virgin is one of the guests. She offers a prayer, and then everyone lies down on the couches that surround the tables.

At each course, a taster tries the emperor's food before he eats to make sure it is not poisoned. Then the taster gives a signal, and everyone eats. And what food! Course follows course as musicians play, singers and dancers perform, and acrobats entertain. It is a wonderful ending to a great holiday!

As the dessert tables are brought in, the emperor stands and lifts his glass. All the guests stand, too, and hold up their glasses. The emperor calls out *"Salve!"* which means "Good health!" Julius, Livia, Julia, and Marcus all say "Salve!" at the same time. They all look at each other and laugh. After they finish eating dessert, the emperor leaves the triclinium. As he goes out, he calls out *"Vale!"* to his guests. This means "Good-bye!" Julia and Marcus say "Vale!" to everyone as they leave the palace. They are tired, but happy to be home in Rome, the greatest city in the world.

ACTIVITY

OIL LAMP

The ancient Romans lighted their homes with oil lamps, in which they burned olive oil. Some of their lamps hung from the ceiling or stood on the floor. However, most were small bronze or clay lamps that stood on tables and could be carried about as needed. Make your own lamp model and use it for decoration.
CAUTION: *Your lamp is only a model, it is not a real lamp. Do NOT burn anything in it.*

MATERIALS

several sheets of newspaper
1 pound (0.5 kg) self-hardening clay, about the size of an orange
resealable plastic bag
craft stick or modeling tool (optional)
pencil
2–3 markers or pens, any colors and of different thicknesses
poster paint in any color (optional)
paintbrush (optional)
jar of water (optional)

1. Spread the newspaper over your work area.

2. Unwrap the clay and break off a piece the size of your thumb. Place this small piece in the resealable bag and seal it.

3. Squeeze the remaining clay in your hands until it is soft and feels warm. Form it into an egg shape. Smooth it with the craft stick or your fingers to remove any lines or holes.

4. Flatten one side of the egg shape to be the bottom of the lamp so it can stand. Place the flat side on your work surface.

5. Pull out one end of the clay to be the spout where the light would be.

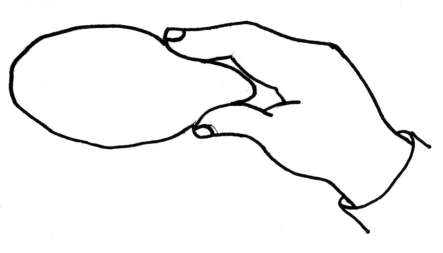

6. Push your thumb into the top center of the lamp to make the container into which oil would be poured. (Do not press your thumb all the way through.)

7. Take out the small piece of clay and roll it between your hands into the shape of a snake.

8. Press each end of the snake shape on the lamp to make the handle opposite the spout. Use the craft stick to smooth the places where the handle joins the lamp, so the handle blends with the lamp.

9. Use the pencil to poke a hole in the lamp at the tip of the spout. Smooth the lamp all over with the craft stick.

10. Use the pencil to scratch a design around the opening of the oil container. Leaving the markers or pens closed, press a design in the clay with their caps. Write your own name or someone else's on the lamp side or bottom. Wash the clay off the pencil and markers as soon as you are done.

11. Leave your lamp on the newspaper to dry—it will stain while it is wet. Let it dry for 2 days indoors, away from radiators, sunny windows, or other sources of heat.

12. When your lamp is dry, paint it if you like. You may want to paint over the names you have written on the lamp, using a different color.

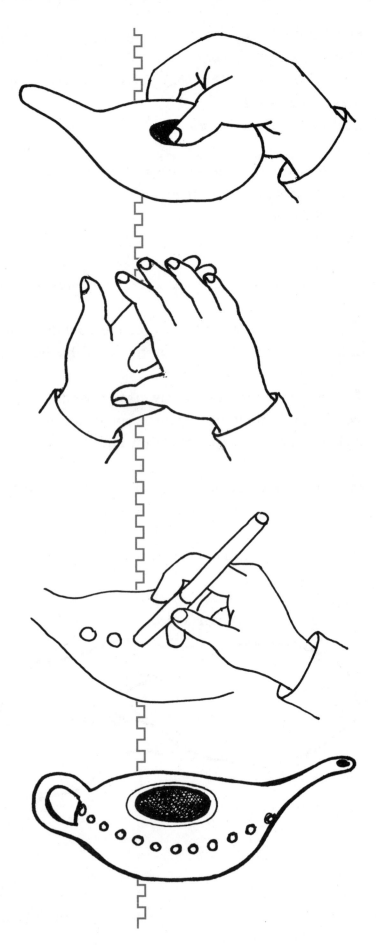

This evening at Emperor Hadrian's palace is the first time that Julia and Marcus have attended a banquet. They know that the emperor's cooks will serve the best food in all of Rome, but they are surprised at how many different dishes there are. Food from all over the world is brought out, one course following another. The cooks have prepared the most unusual foods they can find—including dormice (a rodent) and tongues of small birds called larks. Besides these strange foods, which Marcus doesn't really like, they serve such familiar foods as bread, cheese, eggs, fish, chicken, pork, and many fruits and vegetables. Livia tells Julia that some of the dishes come from a cookbook just written by Apicius (ah-PEEK-ee-oos), a famous food expert.

Men and women dine together in Rome. They lie on couches, facing the dinner table and leaning on their left elbows. One to three guests share a couch. While they eat, musicians play and dancers and acrobats entertain them. Julia notices that the other guests are not too fussy about manners. When they have finished eating, they throw the leftovers on the floor. The emperor's dining room has mosaics on the floor that show bones and pieces of food. The mosaics show what the floor will look like after his guests have finished eating!

ACTIVITY

GUSTUM

The Roman dinner was called **cena**, and the appetizer course was called the **gustum.** The Romans often started their meals with eggs, and ended with fruit. They had a saying, *ab ovo usque ad malum* (ab OH-woe OOS-kway ad MAHL-oom) (from egg to apple), which meant "from beginning to end." Here is the recipe for a simple gustum that you can enjoy today.

This dinner serves four people.

INGREDIENTS

4 lettuce leaves
½ cup (125 ml) ricotta or cottage cheese
2 hard-boiled eggs
12 olives
4 stalks of cooked asparagus
4 slices of cantaloupe
focaccia or other flat bread
½ cup (125 ml) Italian-style salad dressing (oil and vinegar)

TOOLS

4 plates
measuring spoons
table knife
cutting board
4 forks

1. Place a lettuce leaf on each plate. Spoon 2 tablespoons (30 ml) of cheese on each lettuce leaf.

2. Peel the hard-boiled eggs. Use the table knife to cut each egg in half on the cutting board. Cut each half in half.

3. Put two pieces of egg and three olives on each lettuce leaf.

4. Put an asparagus stalk on each plate beside the lettuce leaf. Put a slice of cantaloupe on the other side of the lettuce leaf.

5. Break the bread into four equal pieces. Put a piece of bread on each plate.

6. Pour the salad dressing on the lettuce.

7. Give each person a plate and a fork. Have fun eating your gustum!

ACTIVITY

PRIMA MENSA

The courses in a Roman dinner were called **mensae,** which means "tables." This was because servants brought in the food for each course on a new table, which they placed between the couches on which the diners lay. **Prima mensa** means the "first table," or the main course.

Pork and ham were the meats most commonly eaten. The Romans liked to flavor their meat with all kinds of sauces. Their favorite sauce was **garum,** a salty fish sauce probably like anchovy paste. The Romans were also fond of sweet-and-sour dishes. They added honey and vinegar to garum to make a sweet-and-sour sauce. If you don't like sweet and sour flavors together, you can omit the sauce in this activity.

This dinner serves four people.

INGREDIENTS
½ cup (125 ml) sweet barbecue sauce (An apricot barbecue sauce is best.)
½ cup (125 ml) raisins
4 slices cooked ham
½ pound (0.25 kg) coleslaw
1 cup (250 ml) applesauce

TOOLS
microwave-safe bowl
spoon
oven mitts
microwave oven
4 plates

4 forks
4 table knives
adult helper

1. Pour the barbecue sauce into the bowl. Add the raisins and stir together.

2. Put on the oven mitts. Heat the barbecue sauce and raisins in the microwave oven for 4 minutes on high. Leave the heated sauce in the microwave while you prepare the rest of the meal.

3. Place a slice of ham on each of the four plates.

4. Divide the coleslaw evenly among the four plates. Put the coleslaw on each plate next to the ham.

5. Divide the applesauce evenly among the four plates. Put an equal amount of applesauce on each plate next to the coleslaw.

6. Have the adult helper use the oven mitts to remove the heated sauce from the microwave oven.

7. Spoon an equal amount of the heated sauce and raisins over the ham on each plate.

8. Give each person a plate, a knife, and a fork. Enjoy your prima mensa!

ACTIVITY

SECUNDA MENSA

The **secunda mensa,** or second course, was the dessert table. The ancient Romans enjoyed cakes, custards, puddings, cheeses, and especially fruit. In their desserts they liked the spicy flavor of herbs and spices such as anise, ginger, mint, and thyme. They even used lavender to flavor food! Their only sweeteners were honey and fruit juice—they had no sugar. And no ice cream!

This dinner serves four people.

INGREDIENTS

4–8 fruits from the following list: grapes, figs, dates, apples, pears, melon, blackberries, cherries, and pomegranates
4 servings custard or vanilla pudding, previously prepared
4 gingerbread cookies

TOOLS

colander
large bowl
4 plates
4 small bowls
4 spoons

1. Put the fruit in the colander and rinse it under running tap water. Place the fruit in the bowl.

2. Put a serving of custard in a small bowl in the middle of each plate. Place a cookie on the edge of each plate.

3. Give each person a plate of custard and a spoon.

4. Pass the fruit bowl and allow each person to pick a few pieces. Enjoy your Roman dessert!

WHAT THE ROMANS DRANK

Ancient Romans drank water more than anything else. They particularly enjoyed the water from some special springs. The next most important drink was wine. The Romans always mixed water with their wine before drinking it. At a dinner party, the chief guest decided how much water should be added to the wine. Poor people drank vinegar, also mixed with water. The Romans made a sweet drink called **mulsum** by adding honey to wine. They drank mulsum with the appetizer course. Country people drank the milk of goats and sheep, and sometimes cows. Soldiers in the legions drank beer.

RESOURCES

FOR CHILDREN

John D. Clare, editor. *Classical Rome (Living History)*. New York: Harcourt Brace Jovanovich, Gulliver Books, 1993.

Andrew Langley and Philip de Souza. *The Roman News*. Cambridge, Mass.: Candlewick Press, 1996.

Fiona MacDonald. *First Facts About the Ancient Romans*. New York: Peter Bedrick Books, 1996.

FOR ADULTS

Lesley Adkins and Roy A. Adkins. *Handbook to Life in Ancient Rome*. New York: Facts on File, 1994.

J. F. Drinkwater and Andrew Drummond, editors. *The World of the Romans*. New York: Oxford University Press, 1993.

Chris Scarre. *The Penguin Historical Atlas of Ancient Rome*. London/New York: Penguin Books, 1995.

Jo-Ann Shelton. *As the Romans Did: A Sourcebook in Roman Social History*. New York: Oxford University Press, 1988.

FOR TEACHERS

A journal, newsletter, reviews of new books, and other resources are available from the American Classical League, Miami University, Oxford, Ohio 45056.

FOR EVERYONE

Major museums of art all over the world contain treasures from throughout the Roman Empire. Many college museums contain interesting archaeological finds, such as the important material from Dura-Europus exhibited at the Yale University Art Museum and the Higgins Armory Museum in Worcester, Massachusetts.

GLOSSARY

altar   a table on which the Romans offered sacrifices

amphitheater   an arena with seats all around

aqueduct   man-made water channel

arch   a curved opening in a wall

atrium   an entrance hall in a Roman house

auxiliary   a Roman soldier who lived in one of the countries that was newly added to the empire

ave   Latin for "hail," spoken in greeting to the emperor

Basilica Julia   a courthouse in the forum

boss   the central, raised part of a shield

bulla   a crescent-shaped gold charm worn by children

capital   the top part of a column, on which the roof rests

cena   dinner

centurion   an officer in the legions who was in charge of 100 soldiers

chariot   two-wheeled horse cart

Circus Maximus   Roman racetrack

codex   book

cognomen   a Roman clan name or nickname

Colosseum   the arena in Rome where gladiatorial games were held

Colossus   the huge statue built by Emperor Nero (reigned A.D. 54–68)

column   a pillar used to support a roof or porch

concrete   a mixture of stones set in cement

diphthong   two vowels written next to each other and sounded as one

diptych   a double writing tablet, hinged together like a book

dome   a round roof shaped like half a sphere

emperor   the ruler of an empire

engineer   someone who designs and builds roads and buildings

forum   the central square in Rome and other Roman cities

garum   a salty fish sauce for meat, fish, and vegetables

genius   the spirit of a Roman family, shown as a snake

gladiator   a trained fighter, usually a slave or prisoner, who was forced to fight in the arena

gnomon   the pointer on a sundial

grammaticus   a teacher of Greek and Roman poetry and writing

gustum appetizer

Hadrian (A.D. 76–138) emperor of Rome 117–138

haruspex a fortune-teller who interpreted omens

horologium clock, or sundial

hypocaust a furnace that sends hot air or steam up from the basement through openings in the floor and walls

ides a date in the Roman calendar that fell on either the 13th or 15th of each month

impluvium a pool for rainwater in an atrium

insulae "islands," or apartment houses in Rome

Julius Caesar Gaius Julius Caesar (100–44 B.C.), a great general who ruled Rome 49–44 B.C.

knucklebones an ancient game like jacks played with sheep bones

lararium a shrine for household gods

legions Roman armies

legionary a Roman soldier

litter a device like a hammock used to transport a person

litterator a teacher in an elementary school

macron a mark put over long vowels in Latin dictionaries

mensae Latin for "tables," or courses, at a Roman dinner

mosaic   a design or picture on walls or floors made from small tiles called tesserae

mulsum   wine sweetened with honey

mural   a picture painted on a wall

myth   an ancient story about gods and heroes

nomen   a Roman family name

obelisk   a tall pointed column built as a memorial

omens   signs that were thought to tell the future

palla   a woman's wool cloak

Panis et Circenses   "Bread and Circuses"—the Roman policy of keeping the people happy with free bread and entertainment

Pantheon   the temple in Rome to all the gods

pantomime   a stage performance with song and dance but without spoken parts

papyrus   a reed from which a kind of paper was made

paterfamilias   the oldest male member of a Roman family, who controlled all members of the family

pedagogue   a slave who brought a student to and from school and taught music

pediment   the top triangular front of a building that rises above the roofline

peristyle   a courtyard in a Roman house

praenomen   a personal name of a Roman man

Praetorian Guard   the elite soldiers who guarded the emperor

prima mensa   the "first table," or first course, at a Roman dinner

rhetor   a teacher of speech, law, and politics

rhetoric   the art of speaking or writing effectively

Roman numerals   the Roman way of indicating numbers by letters

sacrifice   an offering made to a god

salve   Latin for "good health," spoken as a greeting

secunda mensa   the "second table," or second course, at a Roman dinner

senator   an elected official who helped govern Rome

shaft   the long body of a column

shrine   a place where Romans worshipped gods

standard   a badge carried by a Roman legion

stola   a woman's tunic with a deep collar hanging down over the shoulders

strigil   a bronze scraper used to clean oil off the body

stylus   a pointed stick used to scratch letters on a wax tablet

tablinum   a study in a Roman house

tesserae   tiles used to make a mosaic

testudo "tortoise," the Roman battle lineup made by overlapping shields

Tiberius (42 B.C.–A.D. 37) emperor of Rome A.D. 14–37

toga a formal robe worn by Roman men and boys

Trajan (A.D. 53–117) emperor of Rome A.D. 98–117

triclinium a Roman dining room

triumphal arch an arch built over a street to honor Roman soldiers who had won a battle

tunica exterior an outer tunic

vale Latin for "good-bye"

Vespasian (A.D. 9–79) emperor of Rome 70–79

Vestal Virgins priestesses responsible for keeping the sacred fire of the goddess Vesta burning

villa a country house

INDEX